CASE STUDIES IN APPLIED
COMMUNITY POLICING

CASE STUDIES IN APPLIED COMMUNITY POLICING

160 201

DENNIS J. STEVENS
University of Massachusetts–Boston

Boston   New York   San Francisco
Mexico City   Montreal   Toronto   London   Madrid   Munich   Paris
Hong Kong   Singapore   Tokyo   Cape Town   Sydney

Editor-in-Chief, Social Sciences: *Karen Hanson*
Series Editor: *Jennifer Jacobson*
Editorial Assistant: *Tom Jefferies*
Senior Marketing Manager: *Judeth Hall*
Production Editor: *Christine Tridente*
Composition/Prepress Buyer: *Linda Cox*
Electronic Composition: *Peggy Cabot, Cabot Computer Services*
Manufacturing Buyer: *Chris Marson*
Cover Administrator: *Kristina Mose-Libon*

For related titles and support materials, visit our online catalog at
www.ablongman.com.

Between the time Website information is gathered and then published, it is
not unusual for some sites to have closed. Also, the transcription of URLs
can result in unintended typographical errors. The publisher would appreciate
notification where these errors occur so that they may be corrected in
subsequent editions.

Library of Congress Cataloging-in-Publication Data

CIP data not available at the time of publication.
    ISBN 0-205-37760-2

Printed in the United States of America

10 9 8 7 6 5 4 3 2 1   07 06 05 04 03 02

*Dedicated to my life-long friend and sister,
Suzi Koller of Woodland Hills, California*

BRIEF CONTENTS

CONTENTS

CHAPTER FOUR

Testing Police Performance in Boston, Massachusetts   44

CHAPTER FIVE
Testing Police Performance in Columbia, South Carolina   62

CHAPTER EIGHT
Testing Police Performance in Midland, Texas   110

CHAPTER NINE
Testing Police Performance in Palm Beach County, Florida   125

FOREWORD

At the dawn of the 21st century, police and the public find themselves joined together in a dance, and they both have sore toes to show for it. They desire each other, but distrust getting too close, and they don't yet have enough practice to bring off the performance smoothly. They are used to being soloists, and find to keep in step they still must warily watch each others' feet.

Most residents of high-crime areas long to form a long-term relationship with the police who serve them. Plagued by street drug markets, loitering gangs, and the sound of gunfire at night, they know they cannot get by without a partner. But too often there is a long history of broken promises and even abuse that needs to be worked through, and this takes a great deal of honest communication. Families with a young male at home have heard tales of seeming harassment, and worry about what might happen to their sons in a "profile" stop. Police who work their neighborhood all live in the suburbs, and know the community mostly through the troublemakers they haul in. The groups that represent the area, especially those claiming "grass roots" connections, have long built their base by challenging police. They rallied their followers around complaints about excessive force and racial or cultural insensitivity on the part of neighborhood officers, and they and the police are on unfamiliar ground now that they meet to discuss joint action plans.

On their side, police have come to recognize that going through the motions without a partner cannot continue. Having one certainly can be aggravating at times, but the taxpayers who pick up the check have developed romantic expectations about their potential relationship with the police, and expect them to embrace them through community policing. For the police, this means that they have to listen to seemingly endless complaints about a broad litany of neighborhood problems, and they are mystified about how they could possibly do anything about them. They fret that local loud mouths will take over, and try to use the police for their private purposes. The many new things that they are being asked to do bring with them many new pieces of paper that must be filled out. They fear that the many hours they are spending on "soft" policing means that they won't "make their stats" with enough arrests or gun seizures, and that they won't make detective as a result. They just want to do what they signed up for, and hope that after the next election this latest fad will fade away.

All of this misunderstanding is compounded by the changing complexion of American cities. The most rapid growth—and often the only population growth at all—is among groups that do not speak English very well, or not at all. These newcomers generally avoid established community churches, and they have difficulty recognizing the value of existing neighborhood organizations. Many come from places where police officers were not the friend of common people, and too often were corrupt and incompetent. They stick to themselves and try to deal with everything on their own. Their children quickly adopt alien ways of life, and risk getting involved in difficulties their parents could never imagine at home. Somehow, police department recruiters never manage to attract them to the force.

This book addresses all of these issues. It roots the practice of community policing in the communities where it has to work, and takes an analytic view of the difficulties involved in making that happen. It is an important link in a grand experiment that the country is undertaking, for it ties the arm-chair theories of policing being promoted by federal funds to the actual work of officers on the street. There are specific lessons that the reader can carry away from this important work on communities and the concept of community policing from an applied perspective which was crafted by my colleague, Professor Dennis J. Stevens, while still keeping an eye on the big picture.

Wesley G. Skogan
Institute for Policy Research
Northwestern University

PREFACE

The centerpiece of this work relates to the new challenges facing police, which are partly due to America's cultural changes and the terrorist alerts putting Western European tradition linked to police policy on notice. Community police strategies can be tailored to meet these new challenges. To help guide this process, 2,010 residents were polled in eight jurisdictions across the United States in English, Spanish, and Chinese, and 76 newcomers to the United States were interviewed in Boston.

This work is linked to *Applied Community Policing in the 21st Century,* a textbook about policing strategies. After evaluating that manuscript, reviewers suggested that a separate book might aid in the organization of my findings. However, what follows is hardly an abbreviated version of the *Applied Community Policing in the 21st Century* and, although not encouraged without the textbook, this book can stand on its own. The organization of this work is simple: Chapter 1 will discuss community police strategies and the design of this investigation, and Chapter 2 will present the collective findings of all eight jurisdictions. Chapter 3 through Chapter 10 will offer the findings of specific jurisdictions, and Chapter 11 will offer a brief conclusion. Once you have read this book, you can expect to have a practical as well as a logical grasp of the experiences of diverse communities and police efforts to maintain public safety, reduce the fear of crime, and enhance quality of life experiences within communities. You might conclude that one strategy well suited to 21st century America is the concept of community policing. Also, you should have developed an informed perspective about community police partnerships and their links to social order.

ACKNOWLEDGMENTS

There are always many to thank who make an author look good. Professors Nina Silverstein, University of Massachusetts–Boston, College of Public and Community Service and Xiaogang Deng, Department of Sociology reviewed chapters on measuring policing performance. Ramona Hernandez, College of Public and Community Service translated the survey from English to Spanish. Cuff Ferguson, College of Public and Community Service helped write the section on Columbia, South Carolina and Richard Hines of the Columbia South Carolina Police Department contributed to his work and this text as well.

Colleagues reviewed the social instrument prior to distribution. Included in that list were Jill DuBois at Northwestern University in Chicago, Captain Michael

Masterson at Madison Police Department, and Kurt Kerley, Mississippi State University. Individuals who helped distribute surveys and/or provided information included: Lt. Stephen Dickinson at Palm Beach Sheriff's Department; Lt. Gerald Rudoff at Miami-Dade Police Department; Professor Ellen G. Cohen, Florida International University; Elizabeth Wright, Alexandria, Virginia; Captain Robert Dunford, Commander, Dorchester Boston Police Department; Chief Charles H. Ramsey, Metropolitan Police, Washington DC; Commander Kent Shafer at the Columbus, Ohio Police Department; Chief Francis D'ambra at Matino North Carolina Police Department; Captain Ben Dickie at Metropolitan-Nashville Police Department; Sutham Cheurprakobkit at the University of Texas–Permian Basin at Odessa; Professor Robert Peetz, Midland College; Mike Schneider, Midland College; Midland Hispanic Chamber of Commerce; Jane Hellinghausen, Midland College; Captain Steve Segura and Nancy Boemer-Otis, Sacramento Police Department.

Ten University of Massachusetts Boston students interviewed 76 participants in Boston. Hector Ruiz interviewed 21 immigrant Latinos who were from many countries including Mexico, Colombia, Panama, Guatemala, Brazil, El Salvador, Honduras, Venezuela, and Peru. They attended an English as Second Language course at Centro Presente in Cambridge, Massachusetts. Antonio Vera-Cruz conducted 12 interviews of Cape Verde families. Maria Gonzalez and Debra Blandin assisted by Damaris Otero, and one other female officer who wanted to remain anonymous—University of Massachusetts Boston students who were also Latino Boston Police Officers—interviewed 17 community members in Spanish, Portuguese, and French Creole in their police districts of Boston and distributed and collected surveys. University of Massachusetts–Boston students and Boston Police Officers Sergeants Roy Chambers and Stanley Demesmin attended several of the community meetings in Boston, distributed surveys, and conducted 16 interviews for this study. Lynda McGann, a UMass graduate student, partnered with Sergeant Robert Young, Sr. in South Boston and interviewed 10 individuals of color.

University of Massachusetts Boston students, Officer Nadya Marino from Martha's Vineyard PD, Melissa Drischoll, Caroline Randall, and Boston University graduate student Danka Charland served as readers, distributed and collected surveys, and/or keyed data from surveys into a computer grid.

Sociology and criminal justice students at the following universities whose names are unknown also deserve mention: California State University Sacramento; Columbus State Community College, University of Massachusetts–Boston; Boston University; Harvard University; Midland College; University of Texas–Permian Basin, Odessa, Texas; University of South Carolina; and Ohio State University. Also, there were numerous others who wished to remain anonymous and others were unknown but involved in neighborhood associations.

Also, personal contributions were made by Wesley Skogan, Lawrence Sherman, Herman Goldstein, David Carter, and Carl Klockars. Finally, with the inspiration of my friend and colleague, Frank Schmalleger, completing this work was a little easier.

Dennis J. Stevens
University of Massachusetts–Boston

ABOUT THE AUTHOR

Dennis J. Stevens, Ph.D., 1991, Sociology, Loyola University of Chicago; Associate Professor of Criminal Justice, University of Massachusetts–Boston, College of Public and Community Service since 1999. In addition to teaching traditional and non-traditional students, he has taught, counseled, and lectured law enforcement officers at police academies and police stations. He has taught and led group encounters among felons at maximum custody penitentiaries such as Attica in New York, Eastern and Women's Institute in North Carolina, Stateville and Joliet near Chicago, CCI in Columbia, South Carolina, and recently at the Massachusetts women's facility, MCI Framingham. He conducted profile assessments among sexual offenders, most recently child molesters. He is well published in books and articles on subjects that include criminology, corrections, and the police. He is a regular contributor to *Law & Order* and assistant editor for two prestigious journals. Lastly, he is a former group facilitator for a national organization specializing in court ordered sexual abuse counseling for parents and has devoted countless hours guiding physically and sexually abused children.

OTHER BOOKS BY DENNIS J. STEVENS

Corrections Perspectives. (1997). Coursewise

Inside the Mind of a Serial Rapist. (1998). Austin Winfield

Case Studies in Community Policing. (2001). Prentice Hall

Policing and Community Partnerships. (2002). Prentice Hall

Applied Community Policing in the 21st Century. (2003). Allyn & Bacon

Applied Corrections: An Introduction. (2004). McGraw Hill. In Press

CHAPTER 1

COMMUNITY POLICE STRATEGIES AND METHOD OF INVESTIGATION

INTRODUCTION

Once we accept the idea that a public agency such as a police department operates in a larger economic, political, and cultural stage that collectively frames the context in which official action takes place, testing their performance makes sense. Community members or constituents really need to know about agency practices and their effects on other members of the community. Knowing about practices and effects allows constituents to guide agencies through their procedures to meet agency objectives without compromising constitutional guarantees and quality services which reasonably meet community and individual expectations. For some of us, the relationship between a public agency and its constituents might be a little unclear. Thomas Jefferson explained it best in a letter to James Madison: "A society that will trade a little liberty for a little order will deserve neither and will lose both." Expressed another way, in a democratic society, the existence of all public agencies depends on the ability of those agencies to provide goods and services to their constituents without compromising collective or individual freedom, and their constituents must be able to measure those goods and services to see how well those agencies are doing in order to suggest change.

Clearly, a public agency requires reliable input from a responsible source prior to making decisions about ways of continuing quality service. Think of it this way: community police strategies establish the police as professional experts on risk factors simply because the police often have experience with those elements (Ericson & Haggerty, 1997). If organized logically, information about police experience is a valuable resource to others. At least, that's one way some residents view what police know or what police think they know. The police have an obligation to provide reliable and complete information to their constituents. Accepting the challenge, it should come as no surprise that some police agencies have produced significant findings for the public through explicit tests for the past two decades (Stephens, 1996). One example comes from a study provided in part by police personnel, who tested community police initiatives in nine police agencies throughout the United States (Stevens, 2001a).[1] What was recommended at the conclusion of that study was that:

> Herein is one advantage of sound research versus opinion and/or (police) experience. Reliable research contains methodological designs that can often produce dependable predictions while providing a body of knowledge that enlightens policy-makers leading to informed decisions. . . . Guesses, although, often wrapped in experience, which of late, have been referred to as a form of profiling is what places many into harms way. It is important to note that while experience is a vital asset, once it is linked to sound research skills, the prospect for success is greater. Research can complement practical experience in many ways. However, research skills without experience can give rise to spuriousness, invalid findings, unreliable and in some cases unlawful recommendations. Research in the public sector, particularly justice agency research, is far different than research in the private sector recognizing litigation potentials and of more importance, issues of public trust.
>
> Recalling many of the pains experienced by the agencies and their community members in this study, one issue is certain. If they had personnel with sound research skills, the path to success would have been more certain and they would have known where they were when they arrived there. In addition, they could have supported their position or achievements more accurately (much to the satisfaction of advocates and opponents). Therefore, the strongest recommendation flowing from those findings is police agencies should obtain the expertise of a trusted researcher in order to have alternative recommendations that might bring them closer to the values of a democratic society without compromising public safety (p. 256).

Furthermore, the contributions of explicit tests can help police executives do their job in an orderly and efficient manner, bringing the agency closer to its mission. If their mission is couched in a community police approach, then we could take some comfort in knowing that people of the community are helping to govern their own community, a process guaranteed by law.

■ ■ ■ ■ ■ ▬▬▬▬▬▬▬▬▬▬▬▬▬▬▬▬▬▬▬

WHAT IS COMMUNITY POLICING?

Community policing is a preventive approach through an empowered problem-solving partnership of police and community to control crime, reduce the fear of crime, and enhance lifestyle experiences of all community constituents.

WHAT IDEAS WERE INVESTIGATED

A question addressed in this work and asked of 2,010 survey takers and 76 interviewees was: does police practice enhance neighborhood safety issues and provide social order or stability?

ASSUMPTIONS OF THE INVESTIGATORS

It was believed that community police strategies give rise to crime control, reduce the fear of crime, and enhance resident quality of life experiences. It was assumed that if community members, especially culturally diverse members, influenced the decisions of the police, it was more likely that public safety and lifestyle experiences would be enhanced too.

In effect, the community, especially culturally diverse communities, will become more active in policing themselves which includes becoming more responsible for crime and their own quality of life issues. The rationale is that the police cannot and should not be responsible for crime control alone. One way this can be accomplished is through community police initiatives which require decentralization of police command, empowerment of authority to police officers and community members within clearly defined limits, and a new managerial role to that of facilitator as found in Total Quality Management techniques.[2] Police organizations are to emphasize preventative services to their constituents as opposed to reactive services.

GOAL OF TESTING POLICE PERFORMANCE

A practical goal of testing police performance is to ultimately forecast with some degree of certainty that something will happen—something will come from apprehending violators or removing abandoned automobiles or helping kids with their homework. Something might be produced that will enhance the quality of life for community residents and for the police personnel who intersect with community members. In a word, predictability (like a magic ball), and being able to see a little bit of the future can lead us to sound recommendations about the question or problem.

WHY USE EXPLICIT TESTS TO
MEASURE COMMUNITY POLICE PRACTICES?

Once we accept the changing nature of police departments and the communities they serve, there are five good reasons (and probably more you can think of) an explicit test[3] is productive in measuring community police practices.

■ ■ ■ ■ ■ ▬▬▬▬▬▬▬▬▬▬▬▬▬▬▬▬▬▬▬▬▬▬▬▬▬▬▬▬▬▬▬▬▬▬▬▬▬

FIVE REASONS EXPLICIT TESTS WORK BEST

- Philosophy of community police initiatives
- Obstacles agencies are confronted with when they develop, implement, and maintain police services
- Personal opinion
- Funding
- Public opinion

PHILOSOPHY OF COMMUNITY POLICE INITIATIVES

Due to the philosophy of community policing and problem-solving commitments, explicit methods of evaluation are necessary to produce appropriate recommendations for change and to bring evidence to its reliability as a police strategy that can enhance quality of life levels for constituents. Counting the number of arrests is not necessarily an appropriate method of ascertaining what changes are necessary or what is working in a police organization to accommodate a philosophy. The fact remains that community policing is not a program. It is not a series of meetings where command advises its audience about police accomplishments during that past month and new responses to criminal activity for the coming months. Furthermore, it is not a meeting under the thumb of the police, rather, control is in the hands of community groups that might include an officer here or there.

A community police approach is an agency-wide way of doing business, different from the conventional hierarchy of command. It is a different style of managerial skills that include the role of a facilitator instead of that of an enforcer because it is a partnership with the community members. It is a priority change from reacting to crime after it happens to that of reacting to crime before it happens or what can be called a preventive approach. It is not the prerogative of the police nor is it their constitutional directive to control crime without community participation and responsibility. Officers and community members must be trained and empowered to resolve their own community problems to enhance public safety and ultimately social order. This relationship seeks mutual trust, respect, accountability, and responsibility. Therefore, cooperation demands some flexibility for the police and balancing of police priorities with the needs of the community.

Since the role of police in this problem-solving partnership is emphasized, measuring their performance is in the best interest of the community and the officers who serve the community (Carter & Radelet, 1999). It comes down to this for the police in the 21st century: should a department wish to provide community police initiatives, they must become decentralized facilitators as opposed to a hierarchy of enforcers.[4] Therefore, measuring the number of arrests might not be an efficient way to verify that community police procedures are maximized. As former Police Chief Dennis Nowicki of Charlotte, North Carolina (1998, p. 265) clarifies, "We no longer want to diffuse a problem, we want to solve it."

OBSTACLES

As with most organizations, there are both inside and outside influences that can impact the quality of police service delivered. Sometimes, those influences can be described as obstacles and explicit tests can aid in offsetting those obstacles.

Inside Police Agency Obstacles: Obstacles occurring inside a police agency include a lack of authority or empowerment among community officers and/or community members to resolve community problems through problem-solving strategies. For example, at a community meeting several vacant homes or buildings are identified as safe-houses for drug traders or drug users. But the participants lack the authority to do anything other than to identify those properties. Certainly, a lack of authority to follow through with solutions affects performance of an officer, morale of the department, and confidence levels of the community.

On the other hand, when officers and community members are empowered to solve community problems leading to crime, but reject their responsibility, similar outcomes might surface. That is, this empowerment issue cuts two ways—command can withhold sufficient authority (and training) and/or authority (or training) when given can be rejected or taken advantage of. In either case, both situations are common experiences among many police departments.[5]

Other internal obstacles might include objections from upper ranking officers who are required to change leadership styles from an authoritative perspective to that of a facilitator (Skogan, 1990). If decision-making guidelines are too broad or too limited or if officers, commanders, and/or community members reject those guidelines, officer and community performance might be greater or lesser than expected.

Yet, how would you know? Through explicit tests, you can get a better understanding about the processes and the relationship between police service and community expectations. Based on the evidence, you could make reasonable recommendations to bring the mission of the department closer to those expectations. It goes without saying that as community problems are resolved through the legitimate initiative of police personnel, trust of the agency grows among residents, social order is enhanced, and some of the roots of crime (abandoned automobiles are removed, street lights are fixed, and gang members are playing sports) are addressed or neutralized.[6]

Then, too, testing relationships between management style changes and management resistance might offer some valuable insights into managerial style transformation, and at the same time reduce police officer stress. These thoughts are consistent with Brodeur (1998) who argues that professional measurement procedures can tell police leaders when a police initiative or a community strategy is meeting goals and expectations.

Outside Police Agency Obstacles: Obstacles originating outside an agency might include political intervention and suspect agendas held by community members and/or civic leaders. Explicit tests could aid in making informed decisions about outside influences especially if confusing knowledge is present. For example, power brokers and/or city officials often influence police practice including the continued employment of police personnel including the chief of police.[7] Sometimes police policy and/or practice oppose political mandates. Drawing on explicit test findings from Midland, Texas (one of the jurisdictions surveyed for *Applied Community Policing in the 21st Century*), participants reported their most serious community problem was a fear or lack of trust of police. However, those survey takers gave police officers and police policy high marks for professional behavior. Why would residents be fearful or have a lack confidence in police practice when they have high regards for police personnel? One answer might be found in yet another investigation:

> Events that led to a less efficient community policing initiative were centered in the priorities of some or several city officials . . . some departments (Camden, NJ and Fayetteville, NC) experienced continual involvement on the part of city officials in police matters whose conduct demonstrated a lack of concern for the welfare of the department (which might well be an appropriate position for officials assuming their priorities are their constituents). However, alienation flowed from the relationship between city hall and the police department because of those political priorities (or at least that's the perception of many commanders). Then, too, some of those officials and inexperienced police leaders supported programs which were standardized items pulled from a shelf much like prepackaged goods in a store, rather than tailored to the specific audience or specific problem.[8]

Midland might be suffering from a similar experience as the agencies discussed above which were Camden, New Jersey and Fayetteville, North Carolina. The city politicians of those jurisdictions dictated police policy and interfered with police operations so much so that those agencies failed to maintain order and failed the officers and the residents, too. It was evident that professional managers and commanders were not in control of those police agencies (although they tried), but political agendas controlled departmental practice. Months after the above investigation was published, the state of New Jersey took control of Camden's municipal structure including the police department. In Fayetteville, many of the top police executives including the chief were squeezed from their jobs. Having a professional compliment of sworn officers including top commander has less to do with crime control, fear of crime levels, and quality of life experiences than expected if political agendas dictate policy. The Camden police department remains a paramilitary operation with the politicians making police policy and the police dictating those policies of arrest, calls, and stops as a method of measuring its success.

Then, too, an explicit test can help support matters concerning accountability. Knowing how well a community is doing its job can be confirmed through an explicit test.

PERSONAL OPINION

One of the rules often violated by most top commanders and community leaders relates to personal opinion or what can be called "subjective" as opposed to "objective" responses. There's good reason why this happens. Policy makers, police managers, and for that matter, you and me, view the world through our own experiences, values, and knowledge as the bases of judging the world.

Other times we might rely on stereotypes or our cultural understanding to help shape our thoughts when we're investigating a question. When police advisers and policy makers are subjective (there is a tendency to prove his or her belief is right), a personal bias can alter the evidence. This, in turn, might ultimately have an effect on public safety issues. For instance, whose idea will be used as a model of social order in a community? Should the police have a different viewpoint than the community, whose notion will be accepted and consequently determine police deployment practices? Police service calls might also be subject to a different set of priorities depending on whose view is considered realistic.

Subjectivity can be described as an ethnocentric perspective. There are two deadly parts to this perspective: first, judging others, and other events on our own set of beliefs. And second, believing that our belief systems and/or judgments are right.

Furthermore, it isn't easy to measure the conduct of others should you use your own experiences and/or culture in part as a way of judging. Now, it's becoming clear that this can be a bigger problem than expected. For instance, if a police officer believes that frightening a status offender (i.e., curfew violator, runaway, and/or truant) with jail will teach the youth a lesson, how often will that officer deny due process rights to a status offender as opposed to helping the child with his or her homework? Sound strange? Maybe. But, some officers use different means to accomplish goals.

Personal opinion or what can be called ethnocentric beliefs can easily bias a policy maker or an investigator's vision and as a result, alter the predictive value of a practice or study's outcome because those unsuspecting individuals believe they need to convince others of their ideals rather than allow the evidence to speak for itself. Objective or professional behavior is difficult because many of us have difficulty leaving our cultural and personal baggage behind. Objectivity means that a policy maker or an investigator must remain nonjudgmental.

FUNDING

Funding today is limited. Brodeur (1998) says there is a lot of competition for federal grant money and city/state funds among police agencies and various municipal agencies for that matter. A quality investigation can indicate best where to spend whatever resources are available.[9] Then, too, there are many expectations about police strategies such as community police strategies. How well did the police meet those expectations? Is community policing reality or rhetoric? For this reason, much of the motivation for conducting assessment is practical, economical, and professionally essential. It is a crucial tool for achieving accountability and for getting value for money in these times of budgetary constraint.

PUBLIC OPINION

Finally, how valid are our thoughts should we neglect to survey the very individuals we are trying to accommodate? Explicit tests of measurements bring to light what the public (or a targeted group under study) has to say about their experiences. They have an opportunity to express their thoughts in a confidential way that might merit immediate attention or lead to a celebration. Ignoring constituent thoughts might be considered a travesty of justice and a little arrogant since the end result of police service is to enhance the quality of life experiences among constituents. Explicit tests help the public learn what the public agency is doing from the perspective of the community. One way to build a trusting relationship with a community is to pay attention to their needs and provide the service they think they are getting. In sum, explicit tests are excellent tools with which to build trust between a police department and the community, learn how well police service is delivered, and learn in what way those services should be changed to provide the quality service expected. And if you're the chief of police, explicit tests are the best way to convince city government that you know what you're doing, and what you're doing is right for the residents. That is, explicit tests are great CYA tools.

WHO SHOULD CONDUCT A
TEST OF POLICE PRACTICES?

Police personnel should conduct explicit tests as opposed to outsiders such as consultants and volunteers.[10] This is an interesting thought since government statistics reveal that most police officers may not necessarily have the skills to conduct a valid and reliable investigation, assuming advanced education and evaluative skills are related variables (Bureau of Justice Statistics, 2001). Would this be similar to having correctional officers assessing prison related perspectives? One observation is that kindergarten teachers in public institutions have more requirements for employment than those individuals whom are generally hired to protect and control the lives of many people.[11]

Nonetheless, it is true that police agencies across the country are involved in assessing police performance, and most utilize consultants and volunteers. For instance, Lincoln, Nebraska, in partnership with a leading polling and consulting organization, developed a telephone survey to collect citizen perceptions of police services. The "Quality Service Audit" was developed as a way to validate a new, success-based talent selection system for police applicants and to provide community oriented police officers with relevant feedback about the quality of their contact with citizens.

Eventually, the Lincoln Police Department used new recruit officers to conduct the interviews by telephone. In this way those recruits became familiar with the department performance indicators and citizen expectations of service more efficiently than in riding along in a police cruiser. Each officer conducted approximately 100 interviews in an eighteen week period calling citizens who had received a citation, been involved in a traffic accident, and/or reported being the victim of a crime (Citta, 1996). Lincoln Police leaders used the feedback to identify and improve departmental systems and procedures that might have been barriers to delivering quality service and to determine training that helped elevate officer performance.

The media or the literature—whichever term you prefer—routinely reports a greater number of examples of explicit techniques conducted to provide police leaders with data about their partnership outcomes, but many departments utilized consultants and volunteers. For instance:

> Columbus Ohio Police Department developed and conducted an extensive survey of its citizens to determine how community policing should be implemented, what its objectives should be, and how it could be maintained. Because of those efforts, community participation was greater than expected when community policing was instituted in the city. Yet, at the same time, the anticipation of success was greatly expected by many individuals that lead to frustration and anger among many policy makers, police command, officers, and community members. (personal communication with Commander, 2000)

> In an analysis of 15 Texas police agencies employing general survey methods, 10 agencies were administering mail surveys to measure attitudes of residents toward local police service, but only one had extended the scope of the survey to identify neighborhood problems. (Surveys of Citizen Attitudes, 1995)

> Surveys in the Reno, Nevada Police Department served as report cards from residents about police performance and image, extent of citizen fear, concerns about crime and quality of contact with department members. In the Peppermill Pop Project, for instance, residents, business owners, and property managers were asked to identify the number one crime problem; whether it could be solved or reduced; and what they could do to improve the neighborhood. (Kirkland & Glensor, 1992)

The St. Petersburg, Florida Police Department used a community-wide survey to identify citizen perceptions of neighborhood problems since 1991. Their survey instrument
measured citizen perceptions on a variety of quality of life indicators and quality of
police service (professional conduct, helpfulness, concern, etc.). Comparing 1994 survey results to 1991's baseline, St. Petersburg police leaders observed significant improvement in resident perceptions on these and other issues. (Stephens, 1996)

Spokane, Washington Police Department, in collaboration with Washington State University, mailed a questionnaire to a random sample of city addresses to assess the
public's attitudes toward police services from 1992 [521 respondents] to 1994 [1,134
respondents]. Results such as improved service; reduced fear of criminal victimization;
and increased citizen interest in working with the police were believed to be evidence
of progress in the department's community policing efforts. The longitudinal survey
also assisted police officers in identifying specific problems by individual neighborhoods and monitored trends over time. (Thurman & McGarrell, 1995)

In March 1994, the Peel Region Police, using an independent marketing research firm,
mailed survey questionnaires to over 10,000 randomly selected citizens. The survey,
which included opinions and attitudes on community safety, police/citizen relationships, and community-based policing, is the most extensive survey effort ever conducted by a Canadian municipal police agency. (Peel Regional Police Survey, 1994)

Decatur, Alabama applied the concept of surveying the city's public housing tenants in
evaluating the department's effectiveness in reducing crime. They asked questions
about residents' fear of crime; impressions of police; opinion of how effective police
were in controlling neighborhood crime; and what problems or concerns should receive priority status. (Dutton, 1998)

THE MADISON STUDY

A study conducted by the Madison, Wisconsin Police Department changed the way
management thought about conducting their own evaluations. After trial and error,
the Madison Police Department (MPD) trained their own personnel to conduct performance evaluations.[12]
    Community policing has been a strategy practiced by the Madison, Wisconsin
Police Department since the early 1980s. Measuring police performance, however,
is a recent experience for them. Masterson and Stevens (2002) describe experiences
of the MPD as the agency measured community policing performance in some of
their challenged neighborhoods. One mission of the MPD was to better understand
the needs of the residents in the neighborhoods through their own experiences. The
MPD could have drawn professionals and volunteers from the University of Wisconsin at Madison.[13] However, what makes their study unique is that measuring

police performance in Madison, Wisconsin was conducted entirely by police personnel.[14] It is the hope of the MPD by reporting their experiences that other agencies will be encouraged to utilize a similar methodological design to measure performance in their communities too, as the advantages far outweigh the disadvantages.

Three lessons were learned from the Madison study. First, by listening to the individuals in the community, the MPD enhanced police decision-making practices that in turn, better served crime control issues through quality police services. Second, the MPD is only one of many participants that shape the meaning of quality police service. That is, it is the voice of their clients, through what they see, hear, and experience that should ultimately influence the levels of police service. Finally, MPD police personnel have greater opportunities to develop community police initiatives and enhance some of their police skills when they conduct the research themselves.

Some of the community problems identified through neighborhood officer initiative included drug and alcohol abuse, low academic performance, lack of employment opportunities and job training, conflict, poor housing and disruptive tenants, inadequate recreational programs, and undeveloped neighborhood leadership. Today, MPD's neighborhood officers are assisted by county social workers, state probation agents, and city building inspectors, all working from the same neighborhood offices. These decentralized networks have allowed the teams to focus on serious neighborhood problems that contribute to the outcomes of crime, dysfunctional families, and social disorder. Many of these notions find congruence with policing experts who argue that the police should not deal with crime alone and they should seek neighborhood participation within a problem-oriented approach.[15]

In the early 1990s, Madison's high crime rate neighborhoods were suddenly hit with the arrival of massive shipments of crack cocaine. As a means to contain the street level violence that became prevalent, the Neighborhood Intervention Task Force was created to supplement the efforts of patrol and neighborhood officers. The mission of the Task Force, referred to today as the Dane County Narcotics and Gang Task Force, was to interdict and prevent trafficking of street level drug sales. In the spring of 1992, the Task Force's efforts were enhanced when the United States Department of Justice recognized the City of Madison as one of 16 Weed and Seed sites. Subsequently, a grant was awarded to help fund and facilitate "weeding out" those responsible for the drugs and violence within the Weed and Seed designated neighborhoods so that "seeding" efforts could occur in hopes of making the neighborhoods once again self-sufficient. The community policing efforts of neighborhood officers was, in theory, to be the bridge between weeding and seeding.

A variety of measures were used to assess and evaluate MPD's Weed and Seed efforts. Hundreds of drug charges and convictions, thousands of dollars in recovered drugs and drug money, seizure of drug houses and assets, and the removal of numerous guns from neighborhood drug entrepreneurs, have been good conventional indicators of taskforce productivity. Yet, something was missing from the evaluation component. Do residents see the same improvements that the MPD sees? Do perceptions differ from one neighborhood to another? Where should future problem-solving strategies be directed? In order to assess resident perceptions, non-conventional evaluation mechanisms were developed including the use of neighborhood officers and police recruits as interviewers. Of course, those officers were trained not by cops but by professional researchers. Consultants and volunteers would have to wait until social order returned to those neighborhoods. True, some members of the community might have been intimidated by police officers asking questions, and there is little support for that thought, nonetheless the results speak for themselves.

The MPD felt that if their challenged neighborhoods became safer and better organized, their residents were more likely to be more outspoken, better educated about issues affecting their lifestyles, and more willing to discuss problems within their community. Also, with their participation also came the opportunity for the department to assume the facilitative role of management at the community meetings and at solving problems since those community members were better prepared to deal with community problems (Skogan, 1998; Stevens, 2001a). There is the thought that if those early studies in the late 1980s were police officers in the field, they could have been able to predict the advent of the huge cocaine problem that engulfed the high-risk neighborhoods in Madison. That is, officers are trained to anticipate problems, and they have a legal responsibility to address anticipations of unlawful conduct; consultants and volunteers are not seen by residents as having either the responsibility or the authority to make things change for the better (Stevens, 2001b).

MADISON AND SOCIAL ORDER

Overall, the MPD believes that social order can be accomplished when community members participate in police decisions. Gaining neighborhood input is best left to police officers since there is much to gain. Compelling evidence has been presented that demonstrates the typical community member would be more honest with an officer than others and that some members of the community who lie about many things would lie or misrepresent to anybody—even a student interviewer. Strong neighborhood associations, their visible and trusted leadership, an active community center, and the active presence of police officers all contribute to a well-informed and involved community that is more likely to identify problems, report them to authorities, and work with the police department to solve those problems. Then, too, officers who are less experienced than others would have an opportunity to learn to rely on some of the information provided by the community and the bridge narrows between the "them and us" or phrased another way, that thin blue line gets thinner rather than bluer.[16] Who should conduct police evaluations? Police officers, but only after being trained by experienced researchers as investigators. With that said let's move on to the investigation at hand.

DESIGN OF THIS INVESTIGATION

There were 2,010 surveys and 76 interviews conducted by participants in different jurisdictions across the USA during the winter of 2000 and the spring of 2001.[17] All participants were surveyed through neighborhood associations, community meetings, chambers of commerce, community policing meetings, public gatherings, and university events.[18] In many cases, most assistant investigators who helped in distributing, collecting, and returning the survey were police officers and/or sheriff deputies who largely worked for the agencies under investigation much like the trained officers in the Madison study. Most of those officers were also current or former university students of the principal investigator. However, you might want to jot down an important point about the participants in this investigation: it was emphasized to all assistant investigators that they should make an effort to survey and interview individuals who were not necessarily "mainstream" community members. That is, survey and interview minorities, people of color, people at the other end of the socioeconomic earning scale, including people who don't speak English, and newcomers.

SURVEY

There was one survey used in this study but several tests were conducted to aid validity.[19] It is estimated that over 7,500 surveys were distributed. One reason for an estimate is that many of the assistant investigators who aided in this project duplicated the survey at their offices located in corporations, universities, police stations, and law academies, and distributed it, without giving the principle investigator (PI) exact totals.

Those assistants mailed or hand delivered approximately 1,245 completed surveys to the PI. The PI added 450 completed surveys to the total after visiting many community meetings in many jurisdictions. Lastly, participants who completed the survey probably at their own homes and/or offices mailed 425 surveys to the PI. Of the 2,120 surveys received, 99 were less than one-fourth completed and 11 were blank or difficult to read and disposed of. Thus, 2,010 were utilized in this survey.

Additionally, the 2,010 surveys produced the results that follow and they will help shape the conclusion in the final chapter, but it goes without saying that findings were offered throughout the sister textbook *Applied Community Policing in the 21st Century*. However, the PI conducted numerous mini-interviews and reviewed many public resources such as websites and newspapers.

Also, assistant investigators in Boston conducted 76 interviews. The interview data will be used to help weigh evidence offered from the surveys in the Boston chapter and will help in future investigations. Those interviews were conducted by ten research assistants, all of whom were under the tutelage of the principle investigator, and all but two males and one woman were born in other countries than the USA such as Cape Verde, Haiti, Dominican Republic, and Guatemala; one was born in Puerto Rico. Seven of the ten assistants were Boston Police officers, and five of the officers were Latinos (four women and one man), including two American males: one an African American and the other an Irish American. Also, two assistants, both Latino males, were engaged in other occupations than police work.[20] Finally, one woman graduate student paired with one of the officers to conduct interviews and to distribute surveys. It is helpful to know who investigators are in order to better understand how they might have obtained data. Results follow.

ENDNOTES

1. See Dennis J. Stevens. (2001a). *Case studies in community policing.* Upper Saddle River, NJ: Prentice Hall. The police agencies evaluated were Broken Arrow, OK; Camden, NJ: Columbus, OH; Fayetteville, NC; Harris County, Precinct 4, TX; Lansing, MI; Nashville, TN; Sacramento, CA; and St. Petersburg, FL. Some of these agencies did little to professionally evaluate their community policing initiatives and as one result, failed often. For some of the agencies that failed, little could have saved them since there were many factors deterring a community policing philosophy. Yet it was believed that those agencies might have been better prepared for their failure had they exercised a professional methodological system to aid them in understanding where the pitfalls were within their city government among their community members prior to initiating a community policing policy.

2. For a closer look at these ideas see David L. Carter and Louis A. Radelet. (1999). *The police and the community.* 6th edition. Upper Saddle River, NJ: Prentice Hall.

3. See the sister textbook of this work for instruction on how to develop an explicit test for police practices: Dennis J. Stevens. (2003). *Applied community policing in the 21st century.* Boston: Allyn and Bacon.

4. See: Skogan, Hartnett, DuBois, Comey, Kaiser and Lovig, 1999; DuBois, & Hartnett, 2001; Stevens, 2002a, 2002b, 1999a.

5. See Carter and Radelet, 1999.

6. See Dennis J. Stevens, 2002a.

7. Part of this section was included in *Applied community policing in the 21st century*

(2003), but due to its relevance and importance to this discussion, it is again mentioned.

8. See Dennis J. Stevens. (2001a). *Case studies in community policing.* Page 259.

9. See Oettmeier and Wycoff (1997) for more detail.

10. See Eck and LaVigne, 1994.

11. See Dennis J. Stevens. (1999a). "Do college educated officers provide quality police service?" *Law and Order,* December, 47(12), 37–41.

12. See Masterson, M. & Stevens, D. J. (2002). The value of measuring community policing performance in Madison, Wisconsin. In Dennis J. Stevens (Ed.), *Policing and community partnerships* (pp. 77–92). Upper Saddle River, NJ: Prentice Hall; and Masterson, M., & Stevens, D. J. (2001, December). Madison speaks up: Measuring community policing performance. *Law and Order, 49(10),* 98–100.

13. The University of Wisconsin is the home of retired professor emeritus and one of the architects of community policing, Herman Goldstein.

14. Captain Michael F. Masterson provided the leadership for the Madison Police Department to develop, conduct, and evaluate their community policing initiatives. In the interest of sharing information so others may learn, Captain Masterson routinely writes about contemporary police issues, in this case Madison's success of measuring community policing performance.

15. See Goldstein, 1977, 1990; Kelling & Moore, 1999; Stevens, 1999b, 1999c.

16. See Dennis J. Stevens, 2001b, 1999c.

17. See Appendix I for a look at the survey

used in this investigation. And only in Boston were any interviews conducted. Information was learned at other sites, but only through exchanges while engaging in other investigative inquiries.

18. The individuals who distributed and collected the surveys were police officers, university professors, university students, neighborhood association leaders, and concerned community members. The Internet was used to communicate with those individuals more than any other devise other than personal visits by the primary investigator. Often the principal investigator was engaged in ongoing discussions with individuals in many of the jurisdictions studied.

19. Validity can be defined as the degree to which a research instrument, in this case the survey, actually measures what was thought to be measured. For example, a highly motivated student of mine who also happened to be a police chief wore his police uniform and took his survey door to door (while his police cruiser driven by one of his officers followed him down the street). He asked residents how safe they felt since he took the job of chief. He reported that all of the residents felt safer since his arrival. It appears that he was not necessarily measuring the fear of crime, but something else. Since then, I call this type of validity the D'Ambra Effect.

20. In total, the officers conducted 43 interviews, and the two non-officers conducted 33 interviews. But all of these assistants also distributed and collected approximately 230 surveys. All of their work was part of a research assignment related to a university course at the University of Massachusetts Boston, College of Public and Community Service and can be found on-line at: http://www.umb.eduacademic_programs/cpcs.html.

CHAPTER 2

TESTING POLICE PERFORMANCE IN EIGHT JURISDICTIONS

INTRODUCTION

Using the survey shown in Appendix I, 2,010 residents in eight jurisdictions across America completed it in the winter of 2000 and the early months of 2001.[1] Those jurisdictions included Alexandria, Virginia; Boston, Massachusetts; Columbia, South Carolina; Columbus, Ohio; Miami-Dade County, Florida; Midland, Texas; Palm Beach County, Florida; and Sacramento, California.

This chapter intends to offer a simple, yet useful guide to looking at individual attitudes without the use of abstract and/or complicated statistical equations. In fact, complex analysis can easily move a reader away from the integrity of a thought, in part due to a failure to communicate. There is some wisdom in explaining survey findings (and everything else) as simply as possible—even Einstein reduced his complex findings to a simple equation of a few symbols.

The primary question asked at the beginning of this investigation was: Does police practice enhance neighborhood safety issues and provide social order or stability? It was believed that community police strategies gave rise to crime control, reductions in the fear of crime, and enhancements in resident quality of life experiences. It was advanced throughout this investigation that the more community members, especially culturally diverse members, influence police decisions, the greater the likelihood that public safety and lifestyle experiences will be enhanced. Based on the evidence provided by residents and public records,[2] community police practices were suspect in most of the jurisdictions investigated. The hope was that community police practices furthered community safety and lifestyle experiences, but this idea was not entirely supported by the data. The final chapter of this work will offer specific detail gathered from each of the following eight chapters representing the eight jurisdictions measured. This chapter offers an overview.

CHARACTERISTICS OF SURVEY TAKERS

You can locate the number of survey takers in each jurisdiction and their collective characteristics by reviewing Table 2.1. Highlighting some important data: the highest number of participants lived in Boston, and the least number lived in Alexandria. White collar jobs were held by 416 (21%) participants, and 384 (19%) described their jobs as blue collar occupations.[3] The survey takers averaged 44 years of age, 859 were females and 1,124 were males; 987 were white; 294 were black; 355 were Latinos; 160 were Asian/Chinese.[4] Over one-half spoke English at home, 2 of every 10 spoke English and another language; and 284 spoke only Spanish, Portuguese, or an Asian language at home.

SURVEY SUMMARY

Most of the participants attended community meetings,[5] but few engaged in any police or municipal decision-making processes,[6] participants reported.

RATING POLICE BEHAVIOR

Over one-half of the participants rated police behavior as professional. Of course, as with all responses, they varied from jurisdiction to jurisdiction. But, almost one in five characterized police performance as intimidating and/or frightening. They reported their respective police agency was largely ineffective in dealing with neighborhood issues. Grading individual officers in solving problems arising from police calls, neighborhood problems, and police problems, resulted in high grades and in some areas, excellent grades. Despite reports that most of the participants wanted to participate[7] in police decision-making processes especially concerning dispositions of abandoned buildings, use of police force, officer discipline, training, and promotions, most said they were rarely invited to do so and the few who were had little authority in those meetings.

SAFETY

One-third of the participants felt unsafe in their neighborhood and only a very few, depending on their race, felt safer than they had a year ago. When participants were asked about future safety, they reported the neighborhood a year from now would be:

- A better place to live: 400 (20%)
- About the same: 704 (35%)

TABLE 2.1   Characteristics of Sample, N = 2,010

	NUMBERS	PERCENTS*/RANGE
Locales		
Boston	897	45%
Columbia	146	7%
Palm Beach	155	8%
Columbus	181	9%
Miami	212	11%
Alexandria	101	5%
Midland	213	11%
Sacramento	105	5%
Length of Time	13.6	0–71 years
Occupation		
Blue Collar	384	19%
White Collar	416	21%
Retired	183	9%
Student	160	8%
Retail	217	11%
Business Owner	315	16%
Other/Missing	335	17%
Age	44	15–78
Gender		
Females	859	43%
Males	1,124	56%
Race		
White	987	49%
Black	294	15%
Latino	355	18%
Asian	160	8%
Missing	214	11%
Homeland		
Western Europe	343	17%
Eastern Europe	54	3%
Haiti/Dominican/Caribbean	139	7%
Central/South America/Mexico	197	10%
Cape Verde/Cuba	57	3%
China/Asia	69	4%
USA	1,098	55%
Missing	53	3%
Language Spoken Home		
English	1,131	56%
English and another language	430	21%
Only Spanish or Portuguese	284	14%
Other	165	8%

TABLE 2.1   Continued

	NUMBERS	PERCENTS*/RANGE
Residents		
Rented	1,233	61%
Owned	662	33%
Missing/Other	115	6%

*All percents rounded. Missing cases not always included.

- A worse place to live: 652 (32%)
- Not sure about its future: 254 (13%)

SERIOUS NEIGHBORHOOD PROBLEMS

Their most serious community problems were identified as

- Street drug activity
- Home invasion
- Conditions of their neighborhood
- Fear and/or lack of trust of police

A neighborhood's serious problem list varied depending on the jurisdiction surveyed. In five of those jurisdictions, fear and/or lack of trust of police was at the top of the list, and in other jurisdictions it was at the bottom of the list.

SOLUTIONS TO NEIGHBORHOOD PROBLEMS

Their answer: quality police service and quality municipal/state services.[8] To resolve community problems, about one-half of the participants reported police should increase patrols, increase arrests, and the courts should administer severe sanctions against offenders. Youths should be supervised. But, these participants were referring to police intrusion or to offenders who lived outside the community or were temporary residents. By no means were they referring to themselves or their youths—selective enforcement.

Also, there was a consensus that more residents should have an opportunity to become homeowners and new businesses should be persuaded to build in the neighborhood. There was a strong relationship between resident status (renters versus owners) and the fear and/or lack of trust of the police and a willingness to aid in neighborhood problems. Also, officers should be residents of the neighborhoods they patrolled which inferred that the officers should have a cultural perspective similar to the neighborhoods where they worked. Quality policing, as explained, refers to strict, but selective enforcement.

However, almost one-half of the participants reported quality municipal/state services were better solutions. Quality municipal services appeared to be of greater importance in solving neighborhood problems than police services. The consensus was that police have no business in neighborhood problems—that is, the best way to stabilize a community is through the people who live there and through municipal public agencies. In a sense, participants saw little difference between municipal services and police services, but assumed police had some form of control over municipal services such as highway repair, maintained highways, quality schools, and business licenses including apartment building controls. It was also argued that businesses catering to criminal activity such as bars, massage parlors, and poorly run businesses that tolerated public disorder—such as 7-11s that allow youths to hang around—should be closed after a second warning; those business owners' licenses should be revoked and slum building owners should be evicted especially when it concerns abandoned buildings. Those abandoned buildings should be leveled and/or rebuilt into livable dwellings or business properties for local residents. The police were seen as a major influence over each of these situations. In fact, when problems arose in licensing for instance, it was believed that "the cops were involved."

As part of this response, about one-fourth of the respondents reported homeownership as another way of controlling neighborhood problems. However, this conceptual solution meant something different in each jurisdiction surveyed. For example, some of the participants wanted police and/or city management to help gain possession of their communities through private and public investment opportunities. They wanted police leadership to show them how to attract investment dollars, especially home mortgages lenders, in order to purchase their own homes. Those who were not renters also reported homeownership as a method of curbing crime.

In some jurisdictions, homeowners wanted authorities to step in and curb the huge influx of new homebuyers who brought to the community "big city ideas about sex and drugs and crime." Other participants from other jurisdictions wanted their property values to increase as other property values of their city in order to borrow the funds to enhance their homes. Yet, they weren't able to get an equity loan because their homes were in need of repair. Others looked to the police as community leaders and as enforcers of all laws including those laws where the police had little jurisdiction (or training) such as property controls and businesses that cheated them by delivering less than quality products. The Catch-22 was that while many participants saw the police as their government representatives, many also possessed a fear or a lack of trust of police and a larger fear or lack of confidence of municipal management. In a final analysis, community members blame police agencies when other public agencies don't do their job.

OVERSIGHT COMMITTEES AND INFORMATION

 # ONE PROBLEM

Then, too many participants wanted input into police decisions and municipal decisions through oversight committees dealing with issues such as hiring, training, discipline, practice which included use of force and critical incident limitations, priorities, and promotional boards. For the purpose of this work, an oversight committee can be defined as an empowered group of community members overseeing police practices.

They wanted an empowered position on those committees to an extent that their influence was relevant in most cases and unchallenged in other cases.

Participants wanted more information about their neighborhoods. They wanted to know the city workers and police officers that provided services. They particularly articulated the hiring of their "own kind" as municipal workers and police officers or at least individuals who could speak their language and understood and respected their heritage. Yet, women municipal workers including police officers were not as welcomed as males. They wanted to know about official procedures, and one of their greatest concerns was the discipline of abusive workers especially among police officers. Their greatest fear was the use or threat of excessive force during a traffic stop. Their fear of "out of control cops" was equaled by their fear of out of control municipal workers.

COMMUNITY MUNICIPAL SERVICES

Some participants reported police and other municipal and/or governmental agencies such as welfare, housing, corrections, streets, including city, county, and state agencies must work through community committees to resolve neighborhood problems as an empowered team. However in one jurisdiction, participants overwhelmingly wanted the police to take control of municipal agencies because they trusted the police more than their elected officials and had more trust in the police than other city agencies.

Overall, survey takers relied on police help because residents had little contact with housing authority personnel, for example. Redirecting traffic and preserving open spaces would be a state-task that might involve a number of "unknown" agencies. They wanted to take their case to the police and the police could lobby towards completing their wishes. However, there appeared to be the thought that police could do anything including the elimination of slum building owners or the boarding up of abandoned buildings.

SUMMARY

Conceptual community police strategies exist. However, municipal services have more to do with social order and stability than law enforcement, and it isn't enforcement that's an issue but it's how police service is delivered that counts. The oddity of it all is that how well a police agency is doing depends on how efficient other public agencies are since community members view officers as their window to government. The public sees the authority of the police as legal and moral as long as potholes are filled, streets are maintained, schools provide quality education, and officers behave themselves in a professional manner (no favorites). Although reported crime is on the decline, fear of crime and fear and/or the lack of trust of police are on the rise. Also, since most community members do not influence police decision-making processes, so it follows that those who don't or can't attend community meetings are rarely represented in neighborhood matters. What is reflected in the voice of these participants is that community government (an empowered community involved in all public services) is necessary to reduce the fear of crime and to enhance lifestyle experiences.

CONCLUSION

Some police advocates argue that lower crime rates are direct results of police policy in concert with community opinions such as "getting tough on crime." If we listen to the 2,010 participants in this investigation, few were involved in a "get tough on crime" discussion with police agencies let alone influenced any process linked to deployment, mini stations, building and vehicle notification, use of force, priories of calls of service, officer hiring and disciplinary actions, training, and/or promotional decisions. When residents sat on advisory boards, they made no mention of any power relative to those committees. Thus, there appears to be strong opportunity for police as an institution to stabilize community-police relationships through conceptual community policing strategies. One reality that becomes clear is that many police advocates confused the difference between community attendance and influencing police decision making processes. The police saw community meetings as an event where constituents could talk about their problems and learn what the department was doing. Many participants saw community meetings as an activity to socialize and an opportunity to "be seen." They saw police officer presentations as "a necessary evil."

A larger question emerged beyond the scope of this work: if those community members who came forward and interacted with police and completed a survey about police efforts don't participate in a police decision-making process, what of all the individuals who don't interact with police at any level? Who speaks for them? Are their views about social order or their serious problems considered? How does the saying go: squeaky wheels get the grease? But, who speaks for the uninvolved such as the challenged, the aged, the young, and the incarcerated? It reasonably follows therefore that public order or a feeling of safety does not exist at the level official rhetoric claims. Additionally, due in part to the differences between official claims of police and justice agencies and actual practice, there are reservations about the intention of police intervention.

One explanation of the findings about official claims versus actual practice is that police practice hasn't changed—official rhetoric has. Since police practice is orchestrated in Western European notions of law and order which could be characterized as cuff'em and stack'em practices, the thought is consistent with some writers who argue that the real mission of law enforcement is to maintain dominant class interests. Keep in mind, there is little wrong with that idea, and police have served the American public well, all things considered. In this regard, however, policing in a democratic society, as it changes, so too must the practices of the institutions that safeguard and serve a free lifestyle. The purpose of this investigation was to aid us in a broader understanding of those concerns. However, since September 11, 2001, the responsibilities have increased among the police and it goes without saying that the police and the community—all residents in the community must move forward to protect the greater public good.

APPENDIX I: SURVEY

Do not write your name on this survey. It's confidential. Your survey will be seen only by the researcher: Dennis J. Stevens, University of Massachusetts Boston who is evaluating the promises of the police through their community policing efforts. Your input will be compared with other residents to better understand your experiences and your needs. Feel free to mail this survey to me or if you have any questions about it I can be reached at: dennis.stevens@umb.edu or my address is: UMB, 100 Morrissey Blvd. Boston, MA 02125-3393. Thanks.

1. What is the name of the neighborhood and the city you live?

   (neighborhood) _____ (city) _____

2. How long have you lived in this neighborhood? _____

3. Would you briefly describe your occupation? _____

4. In the past year, has your neighborhood become: (Check One Only)

   A much safer place to live _____
   A safe place to live _____
   About the same _____
   An unsafe place to live _____
   A very unsafe place _____

5. If you've had contact with the police in the last year, what was the nature of some of those contacts?

I reported an accident _____ or a crime _____

I was issued a citation _____

I was the victim of a crime _____

I was arrested _____

I was a witness to a crime _____

I was in a motor vehicle accident _____

I was contacted about a problem or disturbance _____

I requested information _____

I attended community policing meetings _____ (where) _____

I was involved in another way with the department (please specify) _____

6. Overall, how would you rate the performance of the officers involved?

Professional _____ Fair _____ Frightening _____ Intimidating _____

If you've remembered their names, please list: _____

7. Based on your contact with police at a crime scene, rate the following:

Item	Excellent	Good	Fair	Poor	Very Poor
Response Time					
Solved the Problem					
Made Me Feel Comfortable					
Helpfulness					
Dress/Appearance					

8. How often do community members help the department make decisions about: (Circle One Choice for Each Item)

Item	Always	Very Often	Often	Seldom	Never
Routine Police Auto Patrol	5	4	3	2	1
Routine Bike/Boat Patrol	5	4	3	2	1
Decisions at Mini Stations	5	4	3	2	1
Building Owner Notification	5	4	3	2	1
Use of Police Force	5	4	3	2	1

Priorities of Calls for Service	5	4	3	2	1
Police Officer Disciplinary Actions	5	4	3	2	1
Police Training Courses	5	4	3	2	1
Officer Promotion Committees	5	4	3	2	1

9. How willing are the residents in your community to work with police addressing problems in the neighborhood?

Very willing	_____
Somewhat willing	_____
Somewhat unwilling	_____
Very unwilling	_____
Don't know	_____
Community members have their own agenda	_____

10. In general, how effective has the department been in responding to problems in your neighborhood? Are they:

Very effective	_____
Somewhat effective	_____
Somewhat ineffective	_____
Very ineffective	_____
Don't know	_____
The police have their own agenda	_____

11. Please indicate how strongly you agree or disagree with the following statements:

	Strongly Agree	Some-what Agree	Some-what Disagree	Strongly Disagree	Not Sure
Police officers should spend more time making personal contacts with neighborhood residents and businesses.	5	4	3	2	1
Police officers should be assigned to a neighborhood on a long-term basis.	5	4	3	2	1
I would like to see officers more involved in community programs such as school activities.	5	4	3	2	1
At community meetings, police talk down to us.	5	4	3	2	1

continued

11. *(continued)*

	Strongly Agree	Some-what Agree	Some-what Disagree	Strongly Disagree	Not Sure
The police listen to our non-criminal concerns and act upon them.	5	4	3	2	1
I feel comfortable contacting the Police Department to make suggestions or complaints against their personnel.	5	4	3	2	1
Making communities safer is a responsibility that should be shared by police, community residents, and business operators.	5	4	3	2	1

12. All things considered, do you think the neighborhood a year from now will:

Be a better place to live _____
Stay about the same _____
Become a worst place to live _____
Not sure _____

13. I would like to ask a few general questions about you and your ideas.

How old are you? _____

14. Do you own _____ rent _____ your residence or live with someone _____?

15. How would you describe your race? _____

16. Which country do you consider to be your homeland? _____

17. Your Gender: Male _____   Female _____

18. What language is usually spoken at home? _____

19. Identify the 3 biggest problems that need to be addressed in your community:

_____

_____

_____

20. In your opinion, what actions should be taken to curb the 3 biggest problems in your community?

_____

21. At community meetings, do folks usually work together?

Most of the time _____ Some of the time _____ Seldom _____ Never _____

22. Would you say that everybody (i.e., elderly, youth, former offenders) in the community is encouraged to attend community meetings?

Most of the time _____ Some of the time _____ Seldom _____ Never _____

23. How often do community members leave meetings with mental "to do" lists?

Always _____ Very Often _____ Sometimes _____ Seldom _____ Never _____

24. How often are the actions to resolve community problems actually developed by the community members?

Always _____ Very Often _____ Sometimes _____ Seldom _____ Never _____

25. How often are police actions talked about at meetings?

Always _____ Very Often _____ Sometimes _____ Seldom _____ Never _____

26. How often are those actions changed to fit the results?

Always _____ Very Often _____ Sometimes _____ Seldom _____ Never _____

27. Would you say the plans made at community meetings concerning crime control is generally:

Practical _____ Impractical _____ Not Sure _____

28. In what way is the community safer since the community started meeting?

_____

29. In what way have the police contributed to a safer community?

_____

30. What would you like to add? _____

_____

_____

ENDNOTES

1. Although this chapter will provide data collective findings on all jurisdictions, the textbook written in connection with this work can help give you a better understanding of this test and the designs used: see Stevens, D. J. (2003). *Applied community policing in the 21st century.* Boston: Allyn & Bacon.

2. Public records included official website pages, newspapers, and other public documents, many of which were archived in city and county governmental agencies.

3. Self-reported blue collar work comprised of responses that were truck drivers, laborers, trade persons, and mechanics. White collar work was characterized as work that was primarily described as administrative or professional duties such as those working as nurses, accountants, manufacturing sales, clerical, teachers and professors, and office workers. Retired selections included the clergy, and student included vocational training, on the job training, a leave of absence from a job to enhance job skills, and individuals who worked in homes such as caretakers and parents. Retail work was characterized as descriptions of jobs in small shops and large supermarkets, and business owners were characterized as individuals who owned hairdresser salons, realtors, and retail businesses such as grocery stores and restaurants. Also, there were missing data including those who were unemployed, worked part time, or were between jobs.

4. When the individual categories do not add up, remember that missing cases are not shown. Participants do not always answer every question and sometimes their answers might be hard to read.

5. Because of the way this question was worded, many respondents reported a trend that was different than expected. That is, although most received the survey while attending a community meeting and often officers distributed and collected the survey, many participants continued to report that their last contract with police was something other than attending a community police meeting. It is assumed that most of the respondents had attended a community meeting of some type or were friends with or related to individuals who attended meetings, otherwise the participants might not have received this survey. Another point of confusion, due to the wording, is that it is unknown if the participants were referring to officers or deputies from their local police agency or officers from some other agency.

6. Those areas included deployment of routine police auto, bike, and boat patrol, decisions on mini stations, building owner notification, use of police force, priorities of calls for service, police officer disciplinary actions, police training, and officer promotions.

7. This finding widely varied from jurisdiction to jurisdiction.

8. Bear in mind the participants wrote a series of answers for this question and many others. Upon reviewing those answers, the principal investigator was often guided by assistant investigators and students engaged in various classroom discussion about those answers. Therefore, the categories used throughout this investigation to explain participant response are conceptual in nature. For instance, home ownership might be used as one way to explain a series of responses, but it might relate to different issues depending on where the participants reside. Also, conceptual categories make lengthy descriptions simpler to explain. However, in each jurisdiction, descriptions follow those conceptual categories. Finally, the words used to explain participant answers were not necessarily the words used by the participants. Their explanations were edited to short common usage words in order to, hopefully, make the message clear without altering their spirit of their meaning.

■ ■ ■ ■ ■

CHAPTER 3

TESTING POLICE PERFORMANCE IN ALEXANDRIA, VIRGINIA

INTRODUCTION

Alexandria, the hometown of George Washington, is adjacent to the District of Columbia. *Business Development Outlook* ranked it as the 5th Best Big City for Doing Business in America.[1] Alexandria is in good company with the other top five cities, in order of ranking, Sunnyvale, California; Raleigh, North Carolina; Madison, Wisconsin; and Seattle, Washington. Also, the city of Alexandria has been selected as one of the "Best Cities for Women Today and Tomorrow" in the February 2000 edition of the *Ladies' Home Journal.* Described as "Cozy Yet Cosmopolitan," Alexandria was the only jurisdiction to receive a perfect score for quality of life in the magazine's listing of top 10 cities nationwide as a result of their survey results.

"I think that this survey confirms what we've already known—that Alexandria has an outstanding quality of life for both women and men," said Alexandria City Manager Vola Lawson. "I was very pleased that the survey projects that Alexandria women in the next 20 years will have the highest per capita income in the country." Survey authors used the following criteria: low crime rate, quality of life, good public schools, well-paying and plentiful jobs, dependable health and child care and a significant number of women in local government.

In 2000, Alexandria's population was approximately 128,283 people, however, its daytime population doubles due to the number of workers and visitors. The demographics of its residents consist largely of 60% white (non-Hispanic), 23% black, 15% Hispanic (all races), and 6% Asian.[2] There were 11,000 children in public schools, and the average single family home cost approximately $260,000 in 2000 with a median family income at almost $80,000.[3]

ALEXANDRIA POLICE DEPARTMENT

Alexandria maintains a modern, highly trained, and well-equipped police department, with an authorized strength of 278 officers as of summer, 2000.[4] The basic mission of the Alexandria Police Department (APD) is to maintain law and order, protect persons and property, apprehend persons suspected of crime, direct and control traffic, investigate traffic accidents, and enforce all state and city criminal laws.

The department is committed to community police; a partnership of police officers and citizens working together to address crime and neighborhood quality-of-life issues. In fulfilling their roles, men and women of the APD are guided by the following values:

■ ■ ■ ■ ■ ▬▬▬▬▬▬▬▬▬▬▬▬▬▬▬▬▬▬▬▬▬▬▬▬▬▬▬▬▬▬▬▬▬▬▬

Human life, integrity, the laws and constitution, excellence, accountability, cooperation, problem solving, and ourselves and our role in the community.

In keeping with the above values, the APD expanded the scope of their Citizens' Police Academy to include the city's youth by launching the Youth Citizens' Police Academy.

YOUTH CITIZENS' POLICE ACADEMY (YCPA)

The Youth Citizens' Police Academy provides the city's youth with an inside look at local law enforcement. The purpose of the academy is to increase understanding between the citizens through education and interaction with members of the APD. The academy gives young citizens the opportunity to learn why the APD "can" and/or "cannot" do certain things. It is hoped the instruction will increase police awareness to dispel suspicions and misconceptions, and to increase police/community rapport through this educational program.

During the one-week curriculum, police managers, police officers, civilians, and volunteers teach students. Students are introduced to a variety of topics including:

1. Tactical operations
2. Search and seizure laws
3. Use of force, firearm training to include the use of a firearm simulator
4. K-9 and special operations demonstrations
5. Internal disciplinary process
6. Criminal investigations
7. Vice/narcotics section
8. Field trip to Alexandria's courts
9. Field trip to a residential police officer's home
10. Other law-enforcement-related topics

SCHOOL RESOURCE OFFICERS

After launching its School Resource Officer (SRO) program in 1999, the APD received a three-year federal grant to add two SROs in the schools. Officers are currently working at George Washington, Francis C. Hammond, and Minnie Howard middle schools, and T. C. Williams High School. As a result, each of city middle and high schools are served by a full-time police officer that promotes open communication and conflict resolution to prevent violence and to aid at-risk students.

DRUG ABUSE RESISTANCE EDUCATION (DARE)

The DARE Program provides a police officer and deputy sheriff to teach a one-hour drug prevention class in each fifth and sixth grade classroom weekly for ten weeks. The course is designed to help students deal with peer pressure, stress, and the consequences of taking risks, and to learn how to develop good support systems and alternatives to drug use.

LAW ENFORCEMENT EXPLORER POST

This club is a subdivision of Boy Scouts of America for young adults ages 14–21 who are interested in a career in law enforcement. The Post enables members to get an inside view of police work and offers leadership and law enforcement training. The Post also provides assistance with public service functions such as traffic/crowd control and child fingerprinting identification programs. Law Enforcement Exploring offers good practical experience and encourages community involvement such as distributing pamphlets and assisting with logistics at parades and other special events.

YOUTH CAMP

The Alexandria Police Youth Camp was founded in 1946. Since then, over 17,000 Alexandria children have spent part of their summer in the country. Camp Grimm (named after Charles Herbert Grimm who was killed in Imo Jima) is situated on 97 acres of land near Kilmarnock, Virginia, on a peninsula bordering Indian Creek which flows into the Chesapeake Bay. The camp is operated by Alexandria police officers. Administrative oversight is provided by the Alexandria City Public Schools. Camp Grimm provides a rustic camping experience to Alexandria children between the ages of 8 and 11. Eight campers live in each frame cabin with their counselor. A central dining hall, looking out on the Bay, allows the entire camp to eat together.

Camp Grimm provides a camping experience free of charge to Alexandria boys and girls. All camp applications are accepted on a first come, first served basis. Weekly camping sessions are coeducational. Camp Grimm is operated as a non-profit venture. It is supported by contributions from individuals, business, civic and social service groups, and a grant from the City of Alexandria.

POLICE ATHLETIC LEAGUE (PAL)

PAL uses public safety volunteers to develop popular programs that allow interaction between police, deputies, fire fighters, and youth in the community in a positive way.

AUXILIARY POLICE OFFICER PROGRAM

Auxiliary Police Officers are unpaid volunteers with limited law enforcement powers who perform operational support (e.g., directing traffic, securing crime scenes) and administrative tasks within the department. Following 275 hours of training, Auxiliary Police Officers are issued uniforms and assigned to patrol or administrative units where they volunteer a minimum of 24 hours a month.

CHAPLAINS PROGRAM

Volunteer chaplains of various denominations schedule their time to ride along with police officers on patrol. They offer counseling and may be called in to counsel an officer involved in a serious incident. They will also accompany an officer on death notifications and provide other services on request.

COMMUNITY ACTION TEAM (CAT)

The Community Action Team is a citizen action group formed in 1970 to provide a communications link between police and community in times of neighborhood unrest.

RESIDENTIAL POLICING

One of Alexandria's most successful components of its community-policing partnership is the Residential Police Officer (RPO) program, in which officers live in the neighborhoods they are assigned to patrol. Officers build relationships with their neighbors, handle calls for service, assist investigators on major criminal cases, and develop specialized programs and solutions to address the needs of residents.

Other APD programs include among others: Crime Prevention Council, Crime Information for New Residents, Civic/Community Association Liaison, Officer Friendly, Ride-a-Long Program, Speakers Bureau, and Volunteers.

SEXUAL ASSAULT RESPONSE
AND AWARENESS (SARA)

This program is outlined in *Applied Community Policing in the 21st Century*. However, The Office on Women's SARA Program provided comprehensive services to 588 survivors of sexual assault during 1999, including 24-hour crisis intervention, individual and group counseling, hospital accompaniment, and criminal justice support and advocacy.

CRIME STATISTICS

In 1999, the total number of Part I crimes reached its lowest point (5,682) in 33 years. The 1999 total of 5,682 is 41% lower than the number of crimes reported in 1980. During this period the city's population has increased to approximately 121,700 (17% higher than the 1980 population of 103,990). Some interesting observations can be made when comparing high and low points for individual crime types during the twenty-year period from 1980 through 1999, as shown below.

- From 1980 to 1999, homicides ranged from a high of 17 in 1981 to a low of two in 1995. There were two homicides in 1999. The 20-year average for homicides is seven per year.
- In 1981, there were 64 rapes. The 1999 total was 22 cases, making it the lowest number in 31 years. The 20-year average for rapes is 48 per year.
- The 1999 total of 158 robberies is a 33-year low. During the 20-year period (1980 to 1999) the high point for robberies was 1982, when 591 robberies were reported. The 20-year average for robberies is 387.
- Aggravated assaults reached a high point of 342 in 1994. The 1999 total was 206, which is the lowest in 40 years. The 20-year average is 285.
- The 556 burglaries reported in 1999 is the lowest number of burglaries in 36 years, when 615 burglaries occurred in 1963. The high point for burglaries during the past 20 years was reached in 1980 with 2,607 break-ins. The 20-year average is 1,316 per year.
- The 1999 total of 4,036 is the lowest number of larcenies in 30 years. During the last 20 years larcenies reached a high point in 1993, when 5,682 thefts were reported. The 20-year average is 4,822 per year.
- From 1980 to 1999, the high point for auto thefts was 1995, when there were 1,183 reports of auto theft compared to the low point of 461 in 1981. There

were 702 reported auto thefts in 1999, making it a 15-year low. The 20-year average for auto thefts is 848 per year.

ARRESTS

The number of arrests for serious crime decreased in 1999, down 8%.[5] Arrests for all crimes, including drug offenses, decreased 7%. Juvenile arrests dropped 12.3% in 1999, with 6% fewer juvenile drug arrests than the previous year. Adult drug arrests also decreased 19% in 1999. There were 14% fewer DWI arrests in 1999.

CIVIC ASSOCIATIONS:[6]
ALEXANDRIA FEDERATION OF CIVIC ASSOCIATIONS

The Alexandria Federation of Civic Associations is a non-profit, non-partisan group dedicated to coordinating the efforts of all of the individual civic associations in the City of Alexandria. Each civic association is invited to send a representative to their monthly meetings. Member associations include:[7]

- Alexandria Civic Association
- Auburn Village Civic Association
- Braddock Station Civic Association
- Brookville-Seminary Valley Civic Association
- Clover-College Park Civic Association
- Coalition for Smarter Growth
- Colecroft Owners Association
- Del Ray Citizens Association
- Eisenhower Valley Civic Association
- Founders Park Community Association
- Holmes Run Park Committee
- Inner City Civic Association
- Lenox Place at Sunnyside Association
- Lincolnia Hills/Heywood Glen Civic Association
- Longview Hill Citizens Association
- Mount Jefferson Civic Association
- North East Civic Association
- North Old Town Independent Citizens
- North Ridge Civic Association
- Old Town Civic Association
- Old Town—Hunting Creek Civic Association
- Pavilion on the Park Condominium Association
- Rosemont Citizens Association
- Seminary Civic Association

- Seminary Hills Association, Inc.
- Seminary Ridge Civic Association
- Seminary West Civic Association
- Southwest Quadrant Civic Association
- Taylor Run Citizens Association
- Upper King Street Neighborhood Association
- Wakefield-Tarleton Civic Association
- Warwick Village Citizens Association
- Watergate at Landmark
- Yates Garden Citizens Association
- 1000 Friends of Alexandria City

It would appear that Alexandria offers a resident a better quality of life experience since city services including its police department are progressive and innovative in many areas. Alexandria promotes the idea that "considering Alexandria's philosophy of citizen involvement and the public service commitment of its elected leaders, this ranking is no surprise," said Alexandria Mayor Kerry J. Donley. "We are truly committed to making sure that Alexandria is a diverse and caring community that meets the needs of all of its citizens." Thus, the question—do they?

TESTING POLICE PERFORMANCE IN ALEXANDRIA

There were 101 surveys completed by residents of Alexandria, Virginia. They reported they lived in Alexandria for an average of 13 years (see Table 3.1). Their average age was 47. Of the participants in this investigation, 15 (15%) largely characterized their employment as a blue-collar job, and 10 (10%) as a white-collar job. Twenty-one (21%) reported that they were retired, 20 (20%) were students, and 9 (9%) worked in the retail business. Finally, 23 (23%) reported they were business owners, and 3 (3%) ignored this question.

There were 50 (50%) female and 49 (49%) male respondents. Largely, 53 (53%) described themselves as white, 28 (28%) as black, 4 (4%) as Latino, 10 (10%) as Asian, and 6 (6%) ignored this question.

When participants were asked about the country they recognized as their homeland, 48 (48%) reported it was Western Europe, 2 (2%) said it was Eastern Europe, and 8 (8%) said it was Haiti, the Dominican Republic, or the Caribbean. Four (4%) reported it was Central America, South America, or Mexico, 20 (20%) said Cape Verde or Cuba, 5 (5%) said China or Asia, and 11 (11%) reported it was the USA.

Concerning languages spoken at home, 59 (58%) spoke English at home, 5 (5%) spoke English and another language. Also, 27 (27%) spoke only Spanish or Portuguese at home, and 10 cases were missing. Finally, 70 (70%) of the respondents rented, 17 (17%) owned their home, and 14 (14%) lived at home with parents or others.

TABLE 3.1 Characteristics of Alexandria, Virginia Sample, N = 101

	NUMBERS	PERCENTS[*]/RANGE
Length of Time	13 years	0–47 years
Age	47	19–70
Occupation		
Blue Collar	15	15%
White Collar	10	10%
Retired	21	21%
Student	20	20%
Retail	9	9%
Business Owner	23	23%
Other/Missing	3	3%
Gender		
Females	50	50%
Males	49	49%
Race		
White	53	53%
Black	28	28%
Latino	4	4%
Asian	10	10%
Missing	6	6%
Homeland		
Western Europe	48	48%
Eastern Europe	2	2%
Haiti/Dominican/Caribbean	8	8%
Central/South America	4	4%
Cape Verde/Cuba	20	20%
China/Asia	5	5%
USA	11	11%
Language Spoken Home		
English	59	58%
English and another language	5	5%
Only Spanish or Portuguese	27	27%
Other/Missing	10	10%
Residents		
Rented	70	70%
Owned	17	17%
Lived with others	14	14%

[*]All percents rounded. Missing cases not always included.

MAKING DECISIONS AND MEETINGS

Rarely had participants from Alexandria reported involvement in any of the decision-making processes conducted by the police.[8] Yet, 68 (67%) respondents reported they would participate in police discussions.

At community meetings, 74 (73%) participants reported community members worked together, and 25 (25%) reported they seldom worked together or they didn't answer the question. Also, 68 (67%) participants reported very often or most of the time neighborhood people were encouraged to attend community police meetings. Three out of every ten reported they sometimes received a to-do list as a result of those meetings. Furthermore, during those encounters or meetings, only 37 (37%) participants were allowed to develop their own problem solving remedies. At many meetings, 57 (56%) participants revealed police monopolized the conversations with enforcement talk, and approximately one-third felt that often previous problem solving plans were changed to fit new findings. Yet, one-half of the respondents said they were sure the solutions coming from problem solving discussions were practical. On the other hand, the other one-half of the respondents reported officer solutions were impractical or they weren't sure or didn't answer this question.

GREATEST NEIGHBORHOOD PROBLEMS

The 101 participants in Alexandria reported their greatest neighborhood problems as:

- Lack of trust of police
- Gangs and juveniles
- Street drug activity
- Parking, traffic, and speeders
- Streets, lights, empty buildings, and graffiti
- Home invasion

Specifically, 26 (26%) participants reported their greatest problem was a lack of trust of the police, and 20 (20%) reported it was gangs and juveniles. Eighteen (18%) reported their most serious neighborhood problem was street drug activity, and 14 (14%) reported it was parking, traffic, and speeders. Fifth place was a tie, whereas 11 (11%) reported streets, lights, empty buildings, and graffiti, another 11 (11%) reported it was home invasion.

REMEDIES

When 101 Alexandria participants were asked how to curb those neighborhood problems, the following responses were offered:

- Quality policing and municipal services
- A variety of actions
- Homeownership and business investment

Specifically, 52 (52%) residents described quality policing and municipal services. Quality services consisted of crime information, police patrols, home purchase controls, and business license revocation.

Violent crime, however, was not a prominent issue among the Alexandria participants primarily because they saw violent crime as an occurrence between people who lived elsewhere. For instance, there were many reports that when the "gypsies came to town each spring on their way from Florida to the upper northeast" they break into homes and con residents of their money. "Crooks and gangsters come to Alexandria to commit crime, but they don't live here," one participant wrote on her survey.

Participants were more concerned with receiving police information than with crime. They argued police communications generally "insulted their intelligence," as one participant put it. It was inadequate, edited down, and inconsistent with what television stations and newspaper reported. Many participants revealed that the police did not report all crimes to the community meeting forums and other designated centers that were designed to "get the news." The department claims that through John Crawford, the Public Information Officer for the APD issues a daily email, but many respondents suggest that they don't believe what he writes nor do they think he includes every crime. For example, one participant mentioned that when John Kloch's (a former city prosecutor and now a judge) house was broken into, it wasn't reported. "I believe that their [the APD's] prime objective is to make the department look good and if that means not reporting crimes then so be it. I think it gives us a false sense of safety," reported one association president.[9]

Participants wanted to know what activities and events were going on in their neighborhoods. They wanted city services to aid them in controlling outsiders who brought lower values and, consequently, crime to Alexandria. For instance, there were many complaints about closing undesirable businesses in Alexandria that included poorly operated businesses and businesses that promoted what they saw as inappropriate sexual orientations such as massage parlors, escort services, and movie theaters. The following statement is a typical statement that can help clarify the kind of action the participants sought from city services:

> We approached our civic association police liaison (community police representative). Told him time and again about . . . 4700 Duke Street. Citizens are concerned because the Fox Chase movie theater is adjacent to this park, (and it) shows X rated movies. The theater is listed on a website that attracts what the West Enders feel is an undesirable element, to the woods/park adjacent to the theater . . . (an) arrest was made of a male from Woodbridge, VA. He was involved in homosexual activity, earlier this year . . . (we are) regarding a city petition to have a city ordnance against X rated businesses. . . .[10]

Participants wanted city government to help them control businesses operated by outsiders who committed or promoted crime.

Also, 25 (25%) survey takers described a variety of different actions that were required to bring neighborhood problems under control, but there was little consensus in this category. Some of those remedies included website sexual offender postings, stricter traffic laws especially among drunken drivers, frequent inspection and enforcement of city codes on buildings, homes, and apartment condominiums, a citywide ban on gun ownership, harsh penalties on weapons violations, and strict immigrant regulation enforcement and deportation.

Additionally, 10 (10%) respondents thought homeownership issues and business investment remedies would solve some of Alexandria's problems. What they meant was that many "non-Americans could buy a home in Alexandria and come and go as they pleased," one wrote. Some respondents were suggesting controls on home purchases. Concerning business investment, some of the respondents thought that too few major businesses were located in Alexandria. It was also suggested that one way to rid the city of poorly run businesses or businesses that lacked a virtuous enterprise such as massage parlors would be to recruit major retailers into the city through tax breaks, employee union moratoriums for a period of time, and free parking for their customers.

In the final analysis of their descriptions, there were many comments about how to solve neighborhood problems, yet those thoughts can be divided into two central themes:

- Police and city oversight committees
- Police and other city departments work together

Almost one-half of the respondents revealed that one way to deal with the problems in Alexandria would be for residents to participate in police and city oversight committees. Their thoughts included input into decision-making processes concerning hires, training, operations (including communication of police involvement), practice, promotions, and disciplinary actions of all its personnel. There was a consensus that police and other city agencies should work together to serve the communities though a committee process comprised of empowered residents and city appointees who represented various departments including the police agency.

SAFETY

When the Alexandria sample were asked how safe it was to live in their neighborhood as compared to a year ago, only 18 (18%) reported it was very unsafe or unsafe, and 31 (31%) said nothing had changed. However, 49 (49%) respondents reported it was safer or much safer in their neighborhood as compared to last year.

POLICE PERFORMANCE RATED

Based on the experience a participant had with police:

- 58 (58%) rated police performance as professional
- 12 (12%) rated police performance as fair
- 12 (12%) rated police performance as frightening or intimidating
- 19 (19%) missing

When survey takers talked about the performance of officers at crime or accident sites, over one-half did not report favorably to this question or simply didn't answer it, nor was there a consensus that officer(s) solved the problem, put them at ease, or were helpful. But, over one-half of the survey takers said the officer(s) were appropriately dressed.

POLICE EFFECTIVENESS

When participants were asked how effective the APD was in responding to neighborhood problems, findings revealed the agency was:

- Effective or very effective: 51 (51%)
- Ineffective: 25 (25%)
- Didn't know: 19 (19%)
- Police had their own agenda: 6 (6%)

What else did respondents think? Eighty-seven (86%) participants thought specific officers should spend more time making personal contact with neighborhood residents, and 95 (94%) thought officers should be assigned to a neighborhood on a long-term basis. Only 25 (25%) thought Alexandria officers talked down to them, but many thought officers listened to their non-criminal concerns. However, 54 (54%) survey takers reported they were uncomfortable in taking their suggestions or complaints to the police, and 14 (14%) sometimes felt comfortable. Yet, most participants felt the community would be safer if police and community worked together.

THE FUTURE

When the participants in Alexandria were asked about the future, they reported, all things being equal, it would be:

- A better place to live: 3 (3%)
- Will stay about the same: 26 (26%)

- A worse place to live: 36 (36%)
- Not sure about its future: 36 (36%)

It appears that many survey takers weren't sure about their future safety in Alexandria or they thought it would be a worse place to live.

SUMMARY

Although participant age and length of time residing in the community is somewhat consistent with the collective sample, other characteristics were inconsistent. Also, race, homeland, and languages spoken showed less diversification than the sample at-large. Although the survey takers were rarely involved in police decision-making processes, most wanted to be. The few who were involved did not develop their own problem solving remedies. Changes that occurred since Alexandria began their community police initiative resulted in officer identity or a belongingness with the community. The most serious neighborhood issues were a lack of trust of police and gangs and juveniles. Violent crime was not a prominent issue as outsiders were seen as criminals. Quality police and city services were ways of curbing neighborhood issues, and one way to provide city services and curb their problems was through committees attended by community membership who were granted authority to participate at an appropriate level. At the core of their plan was information about criminal activities and other events that related to crime. Although it depended on which survey was reviewed, safety was an issue as compared to a year ago, but many rated the performance of police officers as professional, and the APD was rated as an effective agency when it comes to dealing with neighborhood matters such as crime. Many residents felt uncomfortable, however, in taking complaints to the APD. Finally, the future did not look bright for Alexandrian neighborhoods in that many said it would become a worse place to live next year.

CONCLUSION: ALEXANDRIA, VIRGINIA

Based on the evidence of 101 Alexandria residents and the public records of both the city of Alexandria and the Alexandria Police Department, it could be argued that strides were made to provide a community police strategy. Reported crime was curbed, however, the fear of crime today and in the future among this sample was exceptionally high and therefore their daily life experiences were not as comfortable as expected. To answer the primary question under investigation: does police practice enhance neighborhood safety issues and provide social order or stability? It was believed that community police strategies give rise to crime control, reduce the fear of crime, and enhance resident quality of life experiences.

One answer is that the fear of crime was great among this sample and it was anticipated to be worse in another year probably because these participants had little confidence in their police agency. Furthermore, while some of the sample attended many meetings, there was little evidence that any of them influenced police decision-making processes. If those individuals who attend meetings do not influence police decisions, then it is highly unlikely that those who refrain from meetings are ever heard. That is, there was little support that community members regardless of their cultural diversity influenced police at any level, therefore public order was not necessarily enhanced through community police efforts in Alexandria.

The evidence suggests that the participants in Alexandria understood the municipal services and police obligations probably better than participants in the other jurisdictions investigated. These participants demanded more than official rhetoric. They wanted action. And, they wanted to be part of that action. Since they weren't, they felt the police agency and the city government gave them "lip service" and little else. To these participants, the police task of serving and protecting was taken for granted. What they wanted was to break the cycle of official rhetoric, participate in the decision-making process through empowered committees, and add their social values and ideas of virtue to official policy. They were appalled by the misinformation distributed about crime and police practice and interpreted this continual trend as intentional and arrogant.[11] And they were appalled that city government issued licenses to businesses that encouraged criminal and immoral activities counter to the community's social values and virtues. These participants argued that those businesses should lose their licenses to operate in Alexandria and that part of the equation for future licensing should be based on the morality of the community where those businesses operated. Part of their frustration as evidenced by a lack of consensus in any particular response seems to be with their lack of control over formal institutionalized controls such as law enforcement activities and city services.

Recommendations include police and city oversight committees attended by empowered community members who also are granted power of evaluation over their remedies in order for them to experience the fruits of their labor. Equally important, those committees need to be open to the public and actions, decisions, and evaluations must be made public in order to gain community support. It goes without saying that those committee members participating must be trained and they in turn should train others. The real error of the department appears to be under-informing constituents of their activities.

ENDNOTES

1. Source: Alexandria's website is available at http://ci.alexandria.va.us/sitenav/live_alex.html.

2. Source: US Census website: http://census.gov and http://ci.alexandria.va.us/city/annual_reports/report2000/ar2000_statistical_snapshot.html.

3. Source: Alexandria's website: http://ci.alexandria.va.us.

4. Source: Alexandria Police Department's website is available at http://ci.alexandria.va.us/police/.

5. Source: APD.

6. All available at http://www.alex.org/

comm_org/index.html. Many of these organizations distributed the survey that helped measure the performance of the Alexandria Police Department.

7. Some of these associations participated in distributing and collecting and returning the survey used to measuring police performance in Alexandria.

8. Those areas included deployment of routine police auto, bike, and boat patrol, decisions on mini stations, building owner notification, use of police force, priorities of calls for service, police officer disciplinary actions, police training, and officer promotions.

9. Personal communication (e-mail) with the Principal Investigator, March 21, 2001.

10. Personal communication with Principal Investigator via e-mail, April 4, 2001.

11. Although, there is little evidence to support their perspective that this police practice is intentional.

■ ■ ■ ■ ■ ▬▬▬▬▬▬▬▬▬▬▬▬▬▬▬▬▬▬▬▬▬▬▬▬▬

CHAPTER 4

TESTING POLICE PERFORMANCE IN BOSTON, MASSACHUSETTS

BOSTON

Boston is a historic city of contrasts.[1] Ancient red-brick sidewalks twist past handsome Federalist houses on the way to soaring glass towers housing state-of-the-art technology. The sports teams are loved and hated at the same time. Residents are fiercely protective of their neighborhoods and fiercely critical of the public transportation, the government, and the weather. In the harbors of Boston lie both the majestic U.S.S. Constitution, still commissioned to fight America's battles, and scores of sleek white fiberglass pleasure boats. There are tiny restaurants tucked into rosy brick town houses on Beacon Hill and huge restaurants on the dizzying tops of skyscrapers downtown. Food ranges from the most radical of nouvelle chic to down home Cajun.

Boston is a diverse city of neighborhoods. From the North End to Bay Village, Back Bay to the South End, Jamaica Plain to Charlestown, the city shows its diversity of populations, of languages, of foods and philosophies. Immigrants from every corner of the globe live in Boston and they have been reshaped into Americans whose memories and customs enrich the community.

Boston is a city where politics is everyone's hobby, where you can hear six different languages in Filene's Basement in one morning; where the world's largest record store and the stately dome of the Mother Church of Christian Science are in the same neighborhood, and where gilded stone lions and a towering 60-story wedge of glass comfortably rub shoulders. Equally important it's home to freedom, and when history books talk about young America, they talk about Boston. For this is the city where people who wanted freedom and choice and better life chances came. They still do.

The US Census reports that in 2000:

BOSTON POPULATION REPORTS

Boston has 589,141 people; among that population, approximately 55% are white, 25% are black, 15% are Latino (of any race), and 8% are Asians living within almost 49 square miles.

A HISTORICAL CHRONOLOGY

1635: First night watch established.

1788: The word *police* appeared for the first time, designating a specific office, "Inspector of Police."

1822: The Town of Boston became the City of Boston. Increases in the population and in the number of businesses operating created increased demand for police patrol.

1838: Law passed permitting day patrol. City had a Day Police and a Night Watch, which by all accounts operated completely independently of one another.

1852: The metal badges were issued—a six point star made of brass.

1854: Boston Police Department established, structured after the model developed by Sir Robert Peele for the London police force.

1858: Telegraph system completed, linking central office and police stations.

1861: White cotton gloves worn by the officers for the first time. Thereafter, "full uniform" included the wearing of such gloves.

1870: 180 "night walkers" were arrested; most were placed on probation and sent home.

1872: The Great Boston Fire of November 9 and 10, which destroyed 776 buildings. The fire was discovered by a patrolman who was chasing boys on Lincoln Street.

1873: First mounted patrol established.

1883: Department headquarters moved from City Hall to 37 Pemberton Square.

1889: Statute passed providing for right-of-way for patrol wagons and ambulances.

1903: First motor patrol wagon placed in service—a Stanley Streamer touring car operated by a chauffeur; the police officer sat on higher seat so that he could look over area's back fences.

1919: Boston Police Department Strike—1,117 policemen went on strike. The officers were not allowed to return to work and were replaced by new officers who received the benefits the striking officers had tried to obtain; salaries were increased, more frequent days off, and uniforms were furnished at department expense.

1925: New Department Headquarters built at 154 Berkeley Street.

1940: St. Valentine's Day blizzard immobilized the city.

1942: Coconut Grove fire, resulting in the death of 490 people and injury to 166.

1950: Famous Brink's robbery occurred in the Brink's Garage on Commercial Street.

1972: Improved radio communication system placed in service, including 911.

1974: Court-ordered busing began, requiring the deployment of large forces throughout the city.

1978: The Great Blizzard of 1978 hit, immobilizing the city for several days.

1995: Mobile date terminals become operational, allowing for prioritization of emergency calls.

1997: Boston Police Department moves into its current state-of-the-art Headquarters facility at One Schroeder Plaza.

REFUGEES AND IMMIGRANTS
IN MASSACHUSETTS 2000

Footsteps of the earliest Western European settlers in the New World continue to step lively through Boston and the Commonwealth. In the last century, more settlers arrived but those individuals are from other parts of the world. That is, Irish, Italian, and African Americans used to be the predominate groups who laid claim to Boston and the Commonwealth's public services including public safety. All indicators suggested that an exodus was in progress in Massachusetts—a changing population. For instance, in a single year, 146,000 more white residents left Massachusetts than moved there. And, a net influx of 25,000 new people arrived who were nonwhite and Latino.[2]

One conclusion that can be drawn from estimates produced by the US Census[3] and other sources is that there are approximately 11.5 million (5% of total US population) refugees and immigrants residing in the United States in the year 2000. And, there are 1.3 million (21% of total Massachusetts population) refugees and immigrants residing in Boston and the Commonwealth of Massachusetts. Then, too,

Albanians, Brazilians, Cape Verdeans, Haitians, and Portuguese have more than doubled their migration to the Commonwealth.

BOSTON POLICE DEPARTMENT

As one of the oldest police departments in the country, the Boston Police Department (BPD)[4] has a rich history and a well-established presence in the Boston community. The BPD was the first paid, professional public safety department in the country. It was patterned after the model developed by Sir Robert Peele for the London Police force. As of September, 2001 the city of Boston had 2,220 sworn officers[5] and 826 paid civilians who serve approximately 574,283 residents[6] of which 63,300 are public school aged children. The police officer/population ratio is 1 officer for every 259 residents.

BOSTON POLICE DEPARTMENT MISSION STATEMENT

We dedicate ourselves to work in partnership with the community to fight crime, reduce fear and improve the quality of life in our neighborhoods.

Our Mission Is Neighborhood Policing

CRIME STATISTICS

- Violent crime fell in 2000 for the 9th consecutive year
- Since 1990, serious crime dropped 48% (2000)
- Serious crime remains at a level the city had not seen in three decades[7]

However, it should be acknowledged that as of August 2001, there were 43 (YTD) homicides reported in Boston, and there were 39 for the year of 2000.[8] In 2000, yearly crime reported was: 39 homicides, 325 rapes, 2,451 robberies, 4,507 aggravated assaults, 4,051 burglaries, 17,228 larcenies, and 7,269 vehicle thefts.

NEIGHBORHOOD POLICING

The primary community policing strategy used by the Boston Police Department is called Neighborhood Policing. The following letter can be found in departmental brochures available to the general public.

■ ■ ■ ■ ■

Fall, 1999

Dear Neighbor:

The strategic plan outlined in this brochure is the product of many hours of hard work by both members of the Boston Police Department and community partners like you. During the past several months, this team and 16 others like it all across the city have been meeting to set new strategic priorities for the future of our Department. Nearly 500 people have actively participated in this process, which has one goal: to realize our mission of working together with the community to reduce crime and fear, and improve the quality of life in our neighborhoods.

We have undertaken this work because we believe that partnerships between police and the community are essential to effective Neighborhood Policing. Our goal in carrying out the Strategic Planning and Community Mobilization Process in 1999 is to build on, and reinvigorate the partnerships we developed in the first round of planning during 1995–96. The participants set out to deepen the collaborative efforts that have been at the heart of the dramatic crime reductions that have taken place in our city. We've learned that the best solutions to crime and disorder issues often originate from those who are the closest to the problem. As a result, the people who have created this plan, and are now embarked on its implementation, feel a deep sense of ownership of the ideas and programs that are expressed below. Together they have assumed accountability for this plan and the measures they feel will be necessary to make it a success.

The team members who developed this plan, we say thanks for the hard work. To everyone who reads this plan we invite you to contribute to its successful implementation by contacting the team leader whose name and telephone number appears on the front of this brochure to see how you can become involved. Working together, we can continue to make our city the safest it can be in the years to come.

Signed,

Thomas M. Menino   and   Paul F. Evans
Mayor of Boston   Police Commissioner

IMPLEMENTATION OF NEIGHBORHOOD POLICING

With the implementation of Neighborhood Policing in Boston came the need for an improved capacity to identify problems and evaluate services. The BPD, having shifted from reactive to proactive policing, could no longer rely exclusively on reported crime to assess its effectiveness. Rather, the BPD needed a tool to include citizens' perspectives in its day-to-day policy decisions. To that end, the BPD conducted its first bi-annual public safety survey.

In 1999, 2,000 randomly selected Boston residents participated in the Boston Public Safety Survey. Those residents responded to 70 questions relating to neighborhood concerns, quality of life, fear of crime, and police services. Some of the highlights from that survey included:

- Over half of Boston residents rate their quality of life as "high."
- Three-quarters (76%) of Boston residents were willing to volunteer their time to work on public safety issues in their neighborhood.
- During 1999, education replaced crime as the top concern of Boston residents.
- On a scale of one to ten (with one meaning "not at all satisfied" and ten meaning "very satisfied"), Bostonians rated police services as an eight.
- Bostonians noted "car breaks" as the most serious crime-related problem in their neighborhoods.
- Since 1995, fear of crime has dropped fifty-one percent (51%), with nearly eight out of ten residents reporting they felt safe walking alone at night.

Based on these findings, the National Crime Prevention Council suggested that Boston was one of the six leading cities with the largest crime reduction over the past ten years.

In early November of 1999, nearly 500 community leaders from neighborhoods across Boston gathered to celebrate the first phase of "Strategic Planning 1999." Composed of a broad spectrum of both citizens and BPD personnel, this gathering capped thousands of hours of planning sessions that had been held citywide during the previous six months. This important initiative also built on many of the key elements from the BPD's prior community mobilization and planning process during 1995–1996.

Some promising early results were highlighted at the event, as each of the 17 planning teams unveiled their newly customized strategic plans for the coming years. The teams represented each of Boston's 11 police districts, as well as BPD's Bureaus of Administrative Services, Investigative Services, Internal Investigations, and Professional Development, and its Operations and Special Operations Divisions.

Mayor Thomas Menino congratulated team participants for their willingness "to work together to drive down crime and fear." Commissioner Evans also praised and thanked each team and noted that the celebration marked "not an end, but a beginning of the tasks of implementing the goals of each team."

By bringing people together in this manner, the Department's Strategic Planning process acknowledged the effectiveness of police and community partnerships and provided an important catalyst for many of the dramatic crime reductions that have taken place since that time. Those partnerships were expected to continue to be one of their most effective tools in increasing the effectiveness of Neighborhood Policing.

Same Cop Same Neighborhood (SC/SN), an outgrowth of the Neighborhood Policing concept, is one of the cornerstones of Commissioner Evans's commitment to the effective delivery of public safety services to every neighborhood in Boston.

More detail about how SC/SN works can be found in his address to a community meeting further in this chapter.

Several important techniques have been identified as particularly effective in promoting SC/SN success thus far, including:

- Reconfiguring boundaries for police districts and sectors
- Training and education sessions with supervisory personnel
- Identification of potential road blocks and suggestions on how to avoid them by middle managers
- An ongoing dialogue about implementation issues, with assistance from the Boston Management Consortium

As a result of this new management approach, the official website for the BPD reports that beat officers developed their own partnerships with members of their neighborhoods through attendance at community meetings and participation in a growing variety of neighborhood activities and events. This new approach won the 1997 Boston City Excellence-*Managing for Safer Neighborhoods* Award, and has been a useful tool in helping to bring the City of Boston to its lowest level of overall crime in 29 years. Perhaps most importantly, it is also helping officers to gain a greater familiarity with the areas they work in, and gives officers a renewed sense of ownership and participation in the positive outcomes they help to generate for the citizens they serve.

The Safe Neighborhood Initiative (SNI) was established in 1993 as a collaboration of public and private sectors to address public safety and community development issues. For instance, the following agencies make up the main components of Dorchester's SNI:

Massachusetts Attorney General's Office

Suffolk County District Attorney's Office

Boston Police Department

Working with community residents these agencies formed a partnership to address crime concerns in the city's most crime impacted neighborhoods. A unique feature of the SNI is the utilization of Human Service Agencies throughout the community to assist in achieving initiative goals.

COORDINATED LAW ENFORCEMENT

Coordinated Law Enforcement Enhanced prosecution is one of the key components of the SNI. Here's how it works: An Assistant Attorney General and an Assistant District Attorney have been assigned to Dorchester District Court and to Suffolk

Superior Court. These prosecutors work exclusively on court cases that are generated out of the SNI. Each case is screened and followed through the system by the same prosecutor. This process allows for open communication between the prosecutor and members of the community and enhances the impact that community members can have in the prosecution of violent offenders who enter their neighborhood.

The goal of this Coordinated Law Enforcement effort is to address community crime concerns by targeting violent offenders and recidivists operating in the neighborhoods by using multi-agency enforcement and prosecution teams.

NEIGHBORHOOD REVITALIZATION

The process of neighborhood revitalization is fostered by This Neighborhood Means Business, a community based SNI program. The incidence of crime and social and economic distress in a community is mirrored in the deterioration of the business and homes in the area. This Neighborhood Means Business assists neighborhood businesses in moving from survival to success by providing:

- Training and technical assistance to small businesses through a 20-week management course concentrating on accounting, marketing, and business plan development
- Access to small business loans
- Training in accessing permits and interacting with governmental agencies
- Business education as defined by an urban neighborhood context

Abandoned properties have also served as magnets for criminal activity. Their renovation both eliminates this activity and enhances the overall appearance of the community. The Abandoned Properties Project targets abandoned properties through the joint efforts of several city departments and the Office of the Attorney General. A local community development corporation and a private, for profit, low and moderate income housing developer serve as receivers for the properties.

PREVENTION AND TREATMENT

Child Witness to Violence Project:

Young children who live in inner-city neighborhoods are increasingly exposed to violence in their communities. Witnessing these violent acts have direct bearing on a child's school work and social relationships. To assist the community in dealing with this issue the Child Witness to Violence Project of the Boston Medical Center plays an active role in the SNI Advisory board. The project provides the following:

- Training for police officers
- Counseling for children and families
- Consultation to the police department and the community

VIETNAMESE/POLICE COLLABORATIVE
TO REDUCE CRIME AND VICTIMIZATION

Through the SNI, the Community Service Office at District 11 has hired a Vietnamese Liaison and a Vietnamese Outreach Worker. This part of the SNI has been essential to involving the area's newest arrivals, the Vietnamese community, in receiving the services of the SNI. These activities include:

- Educating Boston Police Officers and the Vietnamese community about cultural differences to enhance cooperation around public safety
- Organizing safety information meetings and forums for the elderly
- Providing case management and translation services to Vietnamese residents and their families
- Providing emergency assistance and translation to victims of crimes or accidents
- Assisting Vietnamese-speaking victims and witnesses in their contact with police and the courts
- Educating Vietnamese youth in public safety issues and involving them in public service activities

THE COMMISSIONER ATTENDS A COMMUNITY
MEETING AND REVEALS THE PROGRAM

November 15, 2000: The Meetinghouse Hill Civic Association started their meeting at 7:30 at the First Parish Church in Dorchester. There were approximately 50 people present. Also, the Boston Police Commissioner Paul Evans, District Commander Robert Dunford, and Officers Dennis Rorie, Mike Keaney, and Paul Johnson attended. The local city council person and a liaison for the state senator's office were present. A cultural difference existed between the officers and the participants and between the participants too. That is, some were Latinos based on the language they spoke, some were Chinese, and others were of Irish or Italian descent. The meeting started with the pledge of allegiance, and some information by meeting planners. Officer Rorie presented statistics from the community about arrests. For the next 90 minutes the community members presented accounts about problems in the neighborhood which all seemed to revolve around a large (15 to 30) group of young adults who fight and intimidate and vandalize the community. There was a long discussion about how many times they called 911 with little results. Finally, the

Commissioner addressed the audience. He did so without much opposition for 30 minutes, but then the audience became impatient and began to challenge his thoughts.

The Commissioner said that the strength of the police department was approximately 2,200 (sworn) officers. The BPD added 300 officers in the last eight years, but the department was not up to full strength yet. Another 56 recruits were recently hired and they would report to the police academy in January, 2001. Those recruits would be ready for duty in September, 2001. Attorney General Janet Reno was coming to Boston over the Thanksgiving holiday (2000) to discuss the Same Cop Same Neighborhood (SC/SN) program that the BPD had instituted.

The Commissioner continued suggesting that one of the benchmarks of the SC/SN was accountability and strategy planning. "Same Cop Same Neighborhood is one of the cornerstones" of his commitment to the effective delivery of public safety services to every neighborhood. "Under SC/SN, the same beat officers are assigned to a neighborhood beat, and spend no less than 60% of their shift in that designated beat. The intent of SC/SN is to encourage officers to do more street level problem solving," he emphasized. Using principles of shared accountability and ownership for what happens in the designated area of the officer was already helping officers to promote increased coordination among units within the department as well as with the community as a whole. Work processes and reporting procedures have been redesigned, and new uses are being created for technology. These changes created a mandate for important shifts in the assignment and deployment of personnel.

Commissioner Evans suggested that the community and the police must set goals and objectives. He felt that there must be more organized activities for young people. He clarified that the drug control investigators were decentralized. In the past, they worked from headquarters and were everywhere. Reconfiguration of department decisions and command has changed the organizational structure of the BPD. For instance, there are fourteen drug units across the city, at least one for each district and two drug units downtown. The commissioner looked at Commander Robert Dunford and revealed that the captain was in charge of his own drug unit and that was in the best interest of the district.

The Commissioner added that crime analysis shows that crime was down but that the fear of crime, "surprisingly was up. What are the concerns in each neighborhood? In the 1950s, a survey showed that 54% of the general population in Boston reported that they felt safe. Twenty-five years ago when Captain Dunford and me were patrolling Dorchester, as rookie officers, people seemed as if they were safe. But in 1994, 55% of a sample reported that they felt safe. This shows where we as a department need to be. We need to pull all the resources together and adapt the spirit of the department. If the city decentralizes services (building inspections, and so on) quality of life experiences would be enhanced. For the police to meet their commitment to the community, they need the cooperation of other city departments," the Commissioner stated.

Crime was the lowest it had been in 38 years, but there were blurbs on the charts in February (2000) making it rise a bit. There were two reasons for that. One was that there are approximately 300 people every month getting out of jail. Those individuals would return to their old neighborhoods and conduct business as usual. That needs to stop. We need to sit down with the people from corrections and see which individuals are a danger to our communities and do something about that. We need to sit with the sheriff department, case workers, maybe even the clergy and talk to offenders before they're released. If they're a risk to society we need to figure out ways to change that. "The thing is that many city departments are not cooperating with the police to solve problems," Paul Evans clarified.

At that point many residents wanted to discuss experiences they had around their block. Several talked about a building that was occupied by young gang members. The residents talked about attacks on one street. A young Latino woman said parents should be responsible for their children. She cited a specific case when a youngster threw rocks at cars. She followed the youngster home and talked to the parents. Subsequent situations occurred and she contacted the police. In this case, Captain Dunford and several social agency people went to the youngster's home and confronted the parents. "That's how things should be done," she said.

Several residents said the gangs they talked about were not children but adults. The Commissioner said that he would intervene. He would arrange for a meeting with the captain, members from section eight (housing authority), and building inspectors. They would go to that building in question and do something about it. Many of the residents made their reluctance known and again the Commissioner stated that the city departments needed to decentralize and deal with the citizens much like the police department. He stressed that a task force would look into the matter next week and that he would lead that task force. So what do Boston residents think about the Boston Police Department's performance?

TESTING POLICE PERFORMANCE IN BOSTON

Eight hundred and ninety-seven residents were surveyed (45% of the collective sample), and 76 others were interviewed.[9] Boston was the only jurisdiction where interviews were conducted because assistant investigators were available and the principal investigator was able to guide their activity. Largely, the survey respondents lived in the following Boston Districts: 79 (9%) in Chinatown; 566 (63%) in Dorchester; 87 (10%) in East Boston; 62 (7%) in Roslindale, and 103 (12%) in South Boston (see Table 4.1).[10] Most of the survey participants largely attended community police meetings. However, the 76 individuals who were interviewed had never attended a community police meeting.

Typically, most of the Boston survey takers lived in the city for an average of 15 years and averaged 44 years of age. There were a higher percentage of males than females and 70% of both genders rented rather than owned their homes. Furthermore, almost two-thirds of both groups spoke English at home, but under

TABLE 4.1   Characteristics of Boston, Massachusetts Sample, N = 897

	NUMBERS	PERCENTS[*]/RANGE
Districts		
Chinatown	79	9%
Dorchester	566	63%
East Boston	87	10%
Roslindale	62	7%
South Boston	103	12%
Length of Time	15 years	0–71 years
Age	44	15–78
Occupation		
Blue Collar	204	23%
White Collar	171	19%
Retired	48	5%
Student	57	6%
Retail	136	15%
Business Owner	159	18%
Other/Missing	122	14%
Gender		
Females	319	36%
Males	568	63%
Missing	10	2%
Race		
White	606	68%
Black	97	11%
Latino	65	7%
Asian	49	6%
Missing	80	9%
Homeland		
Western Europe	88	10%
Eastern Europe	43	5%
Haiti/Dominican/Caribbean	32	4%
Central/South America/Mexico	12	1%
Cape Verde/Cuba	11	1%
China/Asia	24	3%
USA	652	73%
Missing	35	4%
Language Spoken Home		
English	589	66%
English and another language	208	23%
Only Spanish or Portuguese	15	2%
Other	85	10%
Residents		
Rented	627	70%
Owned	236	26%
Lived with others	34	4%

[*]All percents rounded. Missing cases not always included.

one-fourth spoke English and another language at home such as Spanish, French Creole, or Cantonese. The average age of those interviewed was approximately 33 years of age, and most of them lived in Boston for an average of 5 years. However, 14 of them lived in Boston for an average of 10 years. There were 40 (53%) females and 36 (47%) males interviewed.

OCCUPATIONS AND GENDER

Two hundred and four (23%) participants described their occupation as blue-collar jobs, and 171 (19%) described their occupation as white-collar jobs. Also, 48 (5%) said they were retired and/or in the clergy, 57 (6%) were students or in vocational training or were individuals who worked in homes as caretakers or parents. Also, 136 (15%) described jobs as work in retail environments, and 159 (18%) were small business owners. Finally, 122 (14%) participants were unemployed, worked part-time, and/or were between jobs.

A clear picture of an occupation linked to the 76 individuals interviewed was unavailable. Largely, the investigators agreed that most of them worked in offices or small shops, were students or in vocational training programs, and/or performed a variety of meager tasks. However, nine of the ten interviewees who lived in Boston for 10 years were employed in white-collar jobs or owned small businesses.

PROFESSIONALISM

Over 62% of the survey takers reported the behavior of the Boston police was professional. A high percent also said they were generally fair in their practices with others. These findings far surpassed a recent national survey conducted by the Harris Poll.[11] But, around one-fourth of the participants said officers were intimidating or frightening. Of those interviewed, most reported Boston officers as intimidating.

SAFETY

Forty-eight percent of the survey takers reported there had been little change in their community concerning safety over the past year. And 22% said it was less safe as compared to last year, and 29% anticipated that next year it would be much safer than today (spring, 2001). Additionally, 27% revealed their future looked brighter, while 30% said things would be worse. These findings could be linked to the findings from the Boston Neighborhood Business Survey conducted in 1999.[12] In that study, 62% of those polled said crime had stayed about the same from the previous year, while 25% said crime decreased. Assuming there is some correlation between crime and safety, and since that test was conducted the previous year, it could be argued that feelings of safety improved from 1999 to 2000. However, fear of crime persisted among many of the survey takers and most of those interviewed. Furthermore, most of those interviewed anticipated a brighter future in Boston.

NEIGHBORHOOD PROBLEMS

The five most serious neighborhood problems reported by participants in Boston were:

Boston, N = 897

PROBLEM	PERCENT[*]
Street Drug Activity	29%
Home/Car BE[**]	20%
Gangs and Juveniles	14%
Streets, Lights, Empty Buildings, and Graffiti	12%
Fear or Lack of Trust of Police	11%
Parking, Traffic, and Speeders	7%
No Problem or Other	7%

[*]All percents rounded.

[**]BE = breaking and entering, or car-breaks (this finding is only consistent in Boston and was rarely offered in other jurisdictions).

It should be noted that the category of fear or lack of trust of police meant that the survey takers had little confidence in the officers conducting their task of public safety as opposed to fearing those officers as participant's reported in all the other jurisdictions except Sacramento. This thought is typified in one participant's note, "they don't have a green light to think for themselves. What's right today is wrong tomorrow. Everything changes all the time with the cops." As for those interviewed, there was a consensus about their most serious problems which were identified as police intimidation and community discrimination. These individuals seemed less concerned with street drug activity, home invasion, gangs, and so on.

REMEDIES

When the Boston participants were asked what action should be taken to curb the most serious neighborhood problems, they reported quality police service and quality municipal service. By quality police service, they wanted, among other things, the police to keep their word. "Stop changing things," was a typical statement written often by the respondents. However, many suggested that "changing things" really meant that "downtown politicians made decisions for the cops," as one respondent wrote. Specifically, they reported the best way to curb neighborhood problems was strict enforcement and punitive action toward violators, especially youths and gangs, and strict enforcement among property owners and business owners who contributed to disorder and crime. But, police enforcement practice was second to city services.

Part of Boston's thinking was that city and/or state agencies such as welfare, housing, corrections, streets, including city, county, and state agencies must work together under police directives to resolve neighborhood problems. The participants reported that cooperation by city agencies was necessary because community members could not reach housing authority personnel. Redirecting traffic and preserving open spaces would be a state-task that might involve a number of "unknown" agencies.

They said that city agencies such as the Boston's housing authority, street department, and business licensing agencies should help solve community problems that led to poor life experiences. Many focused on the Boston Redevelopment Authority and wrote that that agency supported large construction companies and the wealthy, rarely reaching out to the "common person." Abandoned buildings should be leveled and/or rebuild into livable dwellings or business properties for local residents. One clear message was that the residents wanted the Boston PD to enforce laws and to take authority of city agencies to aid in enhancing neighborhood lifestyles. Most of the participants in Boston perceived crime as "criminal intent to harm others" and put slum and business owners into the classification of "criminal." The Boston respondents were less willing than the survey takers of other jurisdictions to enhance their community and they trusted the political leaders far less than the police. Therefore, they wanted the police to assume authority over city agencies. The Boston police had the responsibility of dealing with those issues but not as an outside organization.

Optimally, community members would provide input about neighborhood requirements to the police and the police would provide all of the services of the city. The Boston participants wanted little responsibility or work in committee activities or any activity for that matter. Their concerns were more personal rather than community wide. In part, making a living in Boston probably took precedence over community matters.

They wanted more people to own their homes. Keep in mind that Boston's housing market is one of the highest average-priced home markets in the country.[13] They wanted help getting loans through public investment opportunities. But they also wanted big businesses in their communities.

On the other hand, those interviewed wanted little to do with the police or city departments. They seemed to say that they wanted to be left pretty much alone. Most of those interviewed felt intimidated by police, city workers, and the community at large and felt that if they learned more about the American systems that they could operate and compete at an equitable level with other residents.

SUMMARY

It is ironic that Boston has received a lot of praise from federal authorities for its community police concepts. Boston's (reported) crime rate was significantly reduced over a ten-year period. Boston's sample, however, wanted the police to take control of all city services because they trusted the police more than the politicians, who apparently interfered with police practice, often producing changes in police practice. Home ownership concepts were seen as one of their best answers to solving crime as opposed to enforcement of laws. The Boston residents wanted little responsibility over enhancing their communities. On the other hand, new arrivals and immigrants in Boston felt the police were intimidating and community members discriminated against them. They wanted to learn the American way of life and pull themselves up at their own pace.

CONCLUSION: BOSTON, MASSACHUSETTS

Based on the evidence provided by residents and the public records of both the city of Boston and the Boston Police Department, strides have been made to initiate community police strategies. However, crimes of violence were not substantially controlled, and there are indicators that the fear of crime is pervasive among Boston residents, especially among newcomers and immigrants. Also, the respondents in this investigation saw little chance of that changing.

Quality of life issues seem to be suspect among participants due in part to their uncertainty about their future and lack of influence and confidence over city services including their own personal safety and the futures of their children. Therefore, whether police practice enhances neighborhood safety issues and provides social order might be difficult to answer since it might depend on which district you lived in (of course, that is probably true of most cities). One question that can be answered easily relates to the belief that was held before this investigation was underway, which was: do community police strategies gave rise to crime control, reduce the fear of crime, and enhance resident quality of life experiences? If Boston officials see their strategies as community police strategies then the answer is that crime is not controlled, fear of crime is pervasive, and quality of life experiences are not where the residents want those experiences to be, at this time. Also, while many individuals attended meetings, there was little evidence that they influenced police decision-making processes. Furthermore, most of those individuals at meetings were not necessarily culturally diverse groups of residents.

Before we blame the Boston Police Department for what appear to be inadequacies, here's the reality: there are two partners in a community police initiative, the police and the community. Community members argued that they wanted change, but they rely on police leadership to provide those changes. That is, Boston residents want the Boston police to do the work for them. They saw neighborhood work as an obligation of the police. Furthermore, they perceived that the police should solve neighborhood issues including marginal businesses, abandoned and dangerous buildings, opportunities to find suitable living accommodations and opportunities to purchase homes, and crime issues, especially that of controlling the youth of the neighborhood. They argued the Boston Police "owe it" to the people to serve and protect, but only to "some of the people." Maybe it's the history of the city, the mixture of its population, the love-hate experiences of the rich and famous. But the long time residents want to behave as though they have the right to misbehave, and the new residents expect to be treated with respect. Every city has its own dynamics, and these might well be the dynamics of Boston.

Based on the findings from the interviews as compared to survey data, there seems to be a struggle in the city between those who were of Western European culture origins and those who were not. Of late, discrimination seemed to encompass Latinos and Asians as opposed to only African Americans. However, African Americans, American Hispanics (those born in the contigual United States—which does not include individuals born in Puerto Rico) too, seemed to be discriminating against newcomers in similar patterns that they had experienced or perceived that they had experienced. They learned about discrimination through experience. Apparently, a cycle of discrimination or a cycle of hate does find supporters in jurisdictions where change is profound and communities are uncertain as to their role in those communities.

One realization is that whatever direction is pursued by city government or their agencies, Boston residents will be less likely to be satisfied than if they accepted the responsibility of managing their communities through problem-solving strategies in collaboration with the city services including the police. The task is to move crime control, reduction of fear, and enhancement of lifestyles into the hands of those who will benefit the most, the community members themselves. How? In keeping with block organizing principles as established by a group in St. Petersburg,[14] divide the city into logical sections (as opposed to districts), every section should have a section leader who lives in the section and every block should have a block captain. And then it's a matter of block by block building solidarity and responsibility. In undertaking such a major task, perhaps the police should become more than facilitators. They should be in charge of city services too, in order to be consistent with organizing and delivering city services.

Finally, this group of individuals considered silent, those newcomers and others who do not attend community meetings, should be represented too. They do accept American customs and American law and want to "fit in." They are in Boston to share their expertise, motivation, and fruits of their labor, and in return want to be provided with city amenities that other residents receive which include police protection. But who speaks for them on community matters?

ENDNOTES

1. Source: Massachusetts Historical Commission.

2. Sege, I. (July 23, 1991). "All signs point to Mass. exodus." *The Boston Globe,* page 1. For a closer look at the population changes in Boston and the Commonwealth see The Office of Refugee and Immigrant Health, The Bureau of Family and Community Health, and the Massachusetts Department of Public Health. Refugees and Immigrants. June 2000.

3. See US Census Bureau http://www.census.gov/.

4. The Boston Police Department's home page is on-line at http://www.ci.boston.ma.us/police/. In addition, they have 471 marked patrol vehicles, 438 unmarked vehicles, 94 specialty vehicles, 68 motorcycles, 43 bicycles, 5 boats, 14 horses, 13 canines, 2 bomb disposal vehicles, and they received 593,139 total calls for service in 1999. BPD budget in FYE 2000, $204 million.

5. Sworn officer median age is 41, with an average of 17 years on the job.

6. Living in 48.8 square miles with a density of 11,814 residents per square mile.

7. These figures are tabulated according to the national reporting criteria established by the Federal Bureau of Investigations' Uniform Crime Reporting Program. Available on-line at http://www.ci.boston.ma.us/police/1999%20Annual/23.htm.

8. Ibid.

9. The 76 interviews were conducted by ten assistant investigators in Boston, all of whom were under the tutelage of the PI, and all but three of those assistants were born in countries such as Cape Verde, Haiti, Dominican Republic, and Guatemala; one was born in Puerto Rico. Seven of the ten were Boston Police officers. Four of the seven were Latino women and one was a Latino male. Of the remaining two officers, one was an African American male and the other was Irish American male. Two assistant investigators, both Latinos, were engaged in occupations other than police work, and finally, one American women partnered with the African American police officer.

10. There are 11 districts in Boston. Those districts are defined police service districts throughout the city which are generally defined by specific boundaries and neighborhoods. See this site for more information: http://www.cityofboston.gov/police/district.asp.

11. See BJS. (2001). Respondents' rating of performance of police in own community. Page 109, Table 2.28.

12. Survey conducted by the Boston Police Department.

13. At the time of this writing, January, 2002.

14. See Stevens, D. J. (2001a). *Case studies in community policing* (page 207). Upper Saddle River, NJ: Prentice Hall.

CHAPTER 5

TESTING POLICE PERFORMANCE IN COLUMBIA, SOUTH CAROLINA

A BRIEF HISTORY AND SOME DEMOGRAPHICS

Why Columbia, South Carolina? Because it's a city of more history than most and it seems to be caught in its historic past. For instance, only recently has the Confederate Stars and Bars Battle flag been removed from over their state capital building and only in the last decade has the status of married women been legislated to that of an individual as opposed to marital property. Also, the city and its police agency are known to the principal investigator and those who examined Columbia's police strategies relating to community policing in detail.[1]

Located in the geographical center of the state, Columbia was arguably the first city in the United States, and one of the first cities to have a police department despite claims by cities such as Boston and Georgetown. It is, however, the second planned capital in America. Named for Christopher Columbus after a heated debate in the state's Senate, it was founded March 22, 1786 and was built on a site that was then occupied by the plantations of John and Thomas Taylor. Today, Columbia is the largest city in South Carolina with a population of 116,278.[2] Of that number, 49% are white, 46% are black, 3% are Latino.[3]

CATALYSTS BEHIND COMMUNITY POLICING IN COLUMBIA

Primarily there were five distinct catalysts behind Columbia's community policing initiatives. They can be described as the crime rate, police leadership, church leadership, Federal Comprehensive Communities Program, and the initiatives of Columbia's neighborhoods.[4]

CRIME RATES

In the 1980s and early 1990s, crime increased (see Table 5.1, Kelling, 1998). Using 1984 as a baseline, Part I Index Crimes in 1993 were up by 20 percent, index violent crimes by 60 percent, murder was up by 35 percent, rape by 62 percent, robberies by 49 percent, aggravated assault by 60 percent, property crime rates by 14 percent, larceny by 12 percent, and motor vehicle theft by 59 percent. Only burglary rates dropped during the same period. Between 1989 and 1993, arrests of juveniles increased from 475 to 1,091, or 130 percent. Two thousand and eight acts of interfamily violence were reported in 1993, of which 58 percent were spouse against spouse, 10 percent were parent/guardian against children, and eleven percent were among siblings (Kelling, 1998). Table 5.1 also reports crime data during the 1985–1995 period. In terms of patterns, violent crimes peaked in the city during the early 1990s.

POLICE LEADERSHIP

Chief Charles Austin was instrumental in the late 1990s in creating a momentum and community support that is now the foundation of community policing in Columbia. For instance, in a cooperative effort with the Columbia Housing Authority (CHA), he established a "satellite station" in many of the city's public housing

TABLE 5.1 Unified Crime Report: Columbia, South Carolina

CRIME	1985	1986	1987	1988	1989	1990	1991	1992	1993	1994	1995
Murder per 100,000	12	11	16	8	12.5	22	25	15	22	19	9
Rape per 100,000	67	101	77	103	119	105	94	89	67	100	82
Robbery per 100,000	389	446	396	448	NA	NA	687	595	686	571	697
Aggravated Assault per 100,000	931	956	990	1,197	1,357	1,318	1,202	1,170	1,422	1,350	1,401
Larceny/ Theft per 100,000	6,016	7,418	6,958	7,887	7,110	7,563	7,912	6,529	7,316	7,531	7,559
Motor Vehicle Theft per 100,000	519	563	573	990	1,093	1,154	1,073	516	753	660	841
Population	100,024	100,959	94,320	97,609	95,982	98,052	99,990	99,990	99,929	100,504	104,457

projects, and provided opportunities for Columbia Police Department (CPD) officers to purchase homes in the neighborhoods they patrolled. Through the concept of "shared responsibility," businesses, religious organizations, community service agencies, recognized leaders, and residents stepped forward to aid him. The chief promoted the Columbia's Police Homeowners Loan Program, a program designed to provide affordable low interest loans to police officers in exchange for continuous law enforcement services in targeted neighborhoods. Police officers and their families select the home, and funding is provided to obtain a mortgage of the property. Also, the officers receive a police vehicle marked "community policing" which they can drive home. Those vehicles provide visibility to residents establishing a sense of security where the officer resides. The Boston Police Department has used Columbia's model to develop their own program to encourage police officers to take up residence within their divisions of the city (Ferguson, 2002; Kelling, 1998). Another program supported by the chief is the Police in Chairs for Neighborhoods in Crime (PICNIC). Police officers and residents set up lawn chairs along the illegal commerce route of drug dealers to displace the activity elsewhere. The result was the realization of a mobilization effort unequaled in the history of the city. Therefore, Columbia took a three-pronged strategy toward establishing community policing initiatives:

1. decentralized police services through satellite stations
2. provided financial assistance to help officers to purchase homes in neighborhoods they patrolled and to receive a police vehicle to take home
3. establishment of community outreach programs to mobilize neighborhoods toward problem solving strategies using the churches as one base of leadership

CHURCH LEADERSHIP

Church leaders developed strong links among political leaders and colleges with the help of the CPD and city leaders. They collaborated to rebuild their communities. For example, when the House of Prayer wanted to use its own funds to build housing for the elderly, the city helped them obtain land for a church to build upon. The relevance of the role of the church to community policing is that churches are arenas where many community residents can be inspired by church leaders to participate in civic activities. Chief Austin, a respected minister himself, has the support of civic, community, and church leaders.

FEDERAL COMPREHENSIVE COMMUNITIES PROGRAM

As part of a community policing initiative with the aid of the CPD, the Comprehensive Communities Program (CCP) was developed. CCP is based upon a philosophy of "people helping people" through close collaboration among governmental organizations, representative neighborhood groups, private agencies, churches, and the CPD.[5] At the heart of Columbia's program are three police community mobilization officers. These officers operated from community-based offices. They link police, city agencies, social service agencies, and citizen volunteers with citizens who are experiencing serious neighborhood problems or who create them. Chief Austin embraced the importance of community involvement in policing efforts and provided the following perspective about the challenge of Columbia's current community policing initiatives:

> In Columbia, a quiet evolution is occurring as the posture of law enforcement is undergoing dramatic changes. We must be innovative, proactive and aggressive in our efforts, while remaining ever cognizant of the constitutional and civil rights of those people we serve. It is urgent that our citizens join in and help fight crime. The problems all of us face today require shared responsibility between the community and its policing agency. The challenge is clear. We have a responsibility to identify and accurately interpret problems affecting our communities. And, to accomplish that, our role as police must be that of fellow citizens and community members. Total harmony must exist between us to ensure that we provide services which are consistent with the needs of our community.[6]

Columbia was one of sixteen cities in the United States that received the Bureau of Justice Assistance's (BJA) funding for CCP. The BJA defined two principles:

1. communities take a leadership role in developing partnerships to combat crime and violence
2. state and local jurisdictions coordinate a multi-disciplinary approach to combat crime and violence-related problems, as well as the conditions which foster them

Additionally, the grant mandated a jurisdiction-wide community policing and community mobilization prevention initiative, and programming of the police agency had to be based on an area's needs of youth and gangs, community prosecution and diversion, drug courts with diversion to treatment, and community-based alternatives to incarceration. While much of Columbia's police focused on either strengthening administrative processes or changing organizational structures, the core of Columbia's CCP effort was and is its community mobilization program. In part, CCP initiatives in Columbia had included a variety of activities, such as:

- running rap sessions at area schools
- addressing street problems (e.g., abandoned cars and illegal car repairs, abandoned housing)
- presentations and workshops at schools and community meetings
- training and certification of young girls as baby sitters
- youth employment issues

- managing traffic problems
- sponsoring athletic activities
- organizing boys and girls groups
- counseling problematic elementary students
- developing a community resource and address book for graduates
- training volunteers to help in the neighborhoods

INITIATIVE OF COLUMBIA'S NEIGHBORHOODS

Thirty years ago, many of the city's neighborhoods were written off as viable neighborhoods. Middle class families comprised of whites and blacks fled the areas by 1980s. Those population shifts were a "jolt," suggesting to city officials that unless they paid more attention to those neighborhoods, the entire city would suffer, including downtown which was being revitalized at the time. Concurrently, a neighborhood president said that "neighborhood residents just didn't feel that they had a part in government."

One neighborhood manager developed the Columbia's Council of Neighborhoods (CCN). The CCN was a council made up of presidents of neighborhood groups and associations. Its mission was to find ways to participate in governmental processes such as applying for funds from Housing and Urban Development (HUD) or Department of Justice (DOJ).

In 1985, twenty neighborhood organizations were meeting at city hall.[7] One purpose of the CCN was to gain attention and funds to build the neighborhoods. In 2001, the CCN can be described as a volunteer, community-based umbrella organization that coordinates the activities of seventy city neighborhood organizations. CCN serves as a clearinghouse for information, provides a forum for discussion of neighborhood issues, and fosters the education of neighborhood leadership.[8]

CCN's purpose includes improved communication between diverse neighborhood groups, recognition of common problems, and sharing solutions. The ultimate goal is neighborhood empowerment—giving neighborhoods an effective voice in government. It is governed by a board of directors elected by neighborhood presidents whose organizations are members of the CCN. Any city neighborhood organization can become a member. Each organization, regardless of size, has one vote of equal weight. Neighborhoods define their own boundaries; some are as small as a few blocks, while others cover several miles. Neighborhoods competed unequally for available funds, despite similar needs. CCN now provides a link between neighborhood groups and city officials, enhancing the process of identifying neighborhood problems and setting priorities for solutions.

The original concept was to provide a forum for groups representing low and moderate income neighborhoods to be heard by city officials. As more neighborhood groups sought membership in CCN, its constituent base cut across social and economic lines, resulting in cross-communication and understanding of common problems and solutions affecting diverse neighborhoods. Presently 67,683 citizens benefit from CCNs activities, representing 65% of the city's population.

The most significant challenge is changing the status quo. Establishing lines of communication between affluent communities and low income neighborhoods to discuss common problems is unthinkable in some communities. The concept of citizens with diverse socioeconomic backgrounds advising City Council can be threatening to some. Where neighborhoods are bureaucratically defined, the concept of neighborhood empowerment is unwelcomed by those who suspect an erosion of power. Challenges to a sense of community include resistance to change when people are accustomed to living their own lives, the proliferation of young working couples who are unable to attend meetings, and a shifting constituency fueled by mobility and aging.[9]

Some of the typical activities are reflected in the May 2000 conference at the Holiday Inn in Columbia sponsored by the Richland County Sheriff's Office for neighborhood presidents. They considered solutions to common problems about youth crime, developed plans to reduce neighborhood crime, and prepared for a safe summer. Some of the other examples relating to neighborhood activities include:

- The university neighborhood received a grant from the city council to improve a neighborhood boundary that paralleled the railroad tracks of the Norfolk and Southern Railway. The project included a volunteer clean up of trash and brush along a strip of land adjacent to the railroad tracks.
- The Earlewood Park Angels Youth League Baseball Team, for children aged 2 to 9, was put together with a grant. A second team was also started with grant funds along with six issues of the *Earlewood Newsletter*. The grant paid for registration for the teams.
- Another neighborhood organization received a grant for a program for youths and seniors. The program is co-funded by the Empowerment Zone and Community Incentive Funding. Youth programs include karate, swimming, and baseball.
- An historic area of the city installed Victorian street signs provided through a grant.
- The Farrow Hills Terrace Community was awarded a grant for youth summer jobs and to provide smoke detectors for elderly and disabled residents.
- The Cedar Terrace-Brandon Acres neighborhood received a grant for playground equipment including computer games, bumper pool, softball field, tennis courts, ping-pong, foose ball, a walking trail, basketball court, and movies. Other neighborhoods received grants for summer employment.
- The neighborhood of Cottontown received improvement funds for gateway slips, landscaping, and beautification including a street fountain. Funding included the purchase of a lot for a new Habitat Home.

In addition, the CCN provides workshops on topics ranging from management skills to working with government to personal growth for neighborhood officials. Some workshop subjects include:

- How to organize a neighborhood
- How to recruit and train volunteers
- How to create a newsletter
- Money management for neighborhood associations
- Grant writing
- Youth as future neighborhood leaders
- Dealing with difficult people
- How to affect the political process
- Graffiti busters + downtown revitalization
- How to work with developers
- Group dynamics and effective communication

Based on the above information, it can be inferred that Columbian neighborhoods are well supported by municipal agencies including the CPD.

DIRECTION OF COMMUNITY POLICING INITIATIVES

Kelling (1998) explains that Columbia's commitment to community policing appears to be complete. Implementation was initiated prior to CCP funding ". . . and sustainability is not really a question" (p. 30). Kelling argues that with the department's infrastructure, a variety of creative and innovative police-initiated community outreach programs and police-initiated community organizing activities, and collaborative initiatives among police, social service agencies, schools, and the community, Columbia appears to be on a committed and sustained course of jurisdiction-wide community policing.[10]

The City of Columbia's community policing initiatives have been showcased by the National Institute of Justice in The United States Conference of Mayors's publication entitled, "On the Front Lines: Case Studies of Policing in America," and in other articles. Therefore, the following findings should bring further evidence to this showcased agency.

FINDINGS: COLUMBIA, SOUTH CAROLINA

There were 146 surveys completed by residents of Columbia, South Carolina who reported they lived for an average of 10 years in Columbia (see Table 5.2). Their average age was 45. Among the participants, 18 (12%) largely characterized their employment as blue-collar, and 35 (24%) as white-collar jobs. Twelve (8%) were retired, and 19 (13%) were students. Finally, 25 (17%) said they were business own-ers, and 25 (17%) ignored the question or listed an unknown occupation. There were 99 (68%) female and 40 (27%) male respondents. Fifty (34%) described themselves as white, 12 (8%) as black, 49 (34%) as Latino, 26 (18%) as Asian, and 9 (6%) didn't answer the question.

When they were asked which country best describes their homeland, 52 (36%) reported it was Western Europe, 8 (5%) said Haiti/Dominican Republic/Caribbean, 17 (12%) said Central or South America or Mexico, 11 (8%) reported Cape Verde or Cuba, and 55 (38%) said the USA. Also, 107 (73%) survey takers spoke English at home, 13 (9%) spoke English and another language, and 9 (6%) spoke only Span-ish or Portuguese. Finally, 112 (77%) of the test takers rented and 25 (17%) owned their home. Nine (6%) reported they lived with others.

MAKING DECISIONS AND MEETINGS

Rarely did anyone report an official affiliation or input into any decision-making process conducted by the CPD concerning police service.[11] However, almost all of the survey takers reported that most of the time at meetings everyone worked together.

Also, 113 (77%) participants reported that residents were often encouraged to attend community meetings. Few reported they ever had a to-do list arising from those meetings, and 49 (34%) reported they helped develop a problem solving rem-edy concerning a specific neighborhood situation. But none said their participation was influential or cut across any municipal boundaries. At most meetings, while re-spondents revealed police often monopolized those conversations with enforcement topics, sometimes previous problem solving plans would change to fit new findings. Also, 75 (51%) respondents reported they were sure that the solutions coming from problem solving discussions were practical while only 16 (11%) reported solutions were impractical solutions. Sixteen (11%) said they weren't sure about the outcomes of those solutions.

CHANGES

When Columbia survey takers were asked in what way their community was safer since the community started meeting (as opposed to the participant attending meet-ings), many comments were offered which seemed to fit the following categories:

- Response time of officers was about the same: 24 (16%)
- Officers now felt an identity with the neighborhood: 54 (37%)
- People now helped the police do their job: 43 (30%)
- People who previously remained quiet about crime now talked about it: 14 (10%)
- Didn't know or offered no comment: 11 (8%)

TABLE 5.2   Characteristics of Columbia, South Carolina Sample, N = 146

	NUMBERS	PERCENTS*/RANGE
Length of Time	10 years	1–45 years
Age	45	23–71
Occupation		
Blue Collar	18	12%
White Collar	35	24%
Retired	12	8%
Student	19	13%
Retail	12	8%
Business Owner	25	17%
Other/Missing	25	17%
Gender		
Females	99	68%
Males	40	27%
Race		
White	50	34%
Black	12	8%
Latino	49	34%
Asian	26	18%
Missing	9	6%
Homeland		
Western Europe	52	36%
Eastern Europe	0	0%
Haiti/Dominican/Caribbean	8	5%
Central/South America/Mexico	17	12%
Cape Verde/Cuba	11	8%
China/Asia	3	2%
USA	55	38%
Language Spoken Home		
English	107	73%
English and another language	13	9%
Only Spanish or Portuguese	9	6%
Other/Missing	17	12%
Residents		
Rented	112	77%
Owned	25	17%
Lived with others	9	6%

*All percents rounded. Missing cases not always included.

And of interest, 42 (29%) survey takers reported they didn't know how police contributed to their safety. But, 35 (24%) reported that community members felt a sense of identity or belonging to the community due to community meetings.

GREATEST NEIGHBORHOOD PROBLEMS

The 146 Columbia participants reported their most serious neighborhood issue were:

- Gangs and juveniles
- Street drug activity
- Home invasion
- Fear or lack of trust of police
- Streets, lights, empty buildings, and graffiti
- Panhandlers and prostitutes
- Parking, traffic, and speeders

Specifically, 51 (35%) Columbia residents reported their greatest neighborhood problem was gangs and juveniles, and 31 (21%) said it was street drug activity. Twenty-six (18%) reported it was home invasion, and 16 (11%) reported it was fear or lack of trust of police. Fifteen (10%) reported it was street, lights, buildings, and graffiti, 4 (3%) reported it as panhandlers and prostitutes. Finally, 3 (2%) said it was parking, traffic, and speeders.

REMEDIES

When the Columbia test takers were asked what should be done to curb their serious community problems, the following conceptual categories were offered:

- Quality policing and municipal services
- Youth and gang supervision

Sixty-five (45%) residents said the best way to curb their neighborhood problems would be for the city to provide quality police service and quality city or municipal service. Municipal services were mentioned more often than enforcement services. What the survey takers wanted from city services consisted of health care, public transportation, and quality teachers in their public schools. What they meant by health care included reliable information, assistance with health due to poor diets and prenatal care, diabetes, and sexually transmitted diseases. Public transportation included issues of primarily getting to and from work; however, visits to family members in jail[12] or in state health care facilities, shopping, and visiting friends and relatives were also of concern. School issues included poor teachers and a lack of aid toward unruly children, some who had access to drugs and alcohol and with poor teachers, those activities flourished. School subjects that seemed insignificant or unrelated subjects to their children presented major barriers to relaxed lifestyles. Appropriate supervision for youth when school was not in session was reported often, but their rationale was that if the schools could not provide quality teachers, then after school care takers would be worse. On the heels of city services, police services were mentioned, but only as helpful aids.

Also, 34 (23%) survey takers reported no answer or "other" to this question. Some of those "others" included safety issues of schools such as school equipment, desks, and school fixtures. Information that was unreliable (or misunderstood) about retail store hours, payment schedules for bills (telephone, etc.), and methods to ask for or register complaints when city services were not provided were also issues.

Next, 18 (12%) participants reported that youth and gang guidance (not enforcement) was required in Columbia to help curb neighborhood problems. This thought was a third remedy to curb serious neighborhood problems despite the report that gangs and juveniles were the greatest neighborhood problem. While they wanted juvenile gang members to behave, what they wanted more was for the police to guide their own children rather then to arrest them. If there was a problem with their children, the police should inform parents, and parents would handle the situation. It was clear that most parents did not want the police intruding in the lives of their children.

The community members polled revealed other thoughts that can be divided into two central themes:

- Police oversight committees
- Police and municipal departments work together

Of the Columbia survey takers, 71 (49%) furthered their thoughts about solving their greatest neighborhood problem through police oversight committees. That is, almost one-half of the participants implied that they wanted two things: police information and police oversight influence relating specifically to police conduct. These survey takers, while reporting that Columbia police officers were professional and nonthreatening, wanted information about and power in the CPD decision-making process which included hiring, operations, deployment, use of force decisions, promotions, and training of officers. Community members wanted more control over police officer behavior and policy. In part, this thought could be influenced by the low level of confidence participants held concerning police policy.

Also, 62 (43%) respondents reported police and city departments must work together to provide services to their neighborhood. In this case, participants emphasized services such as health care, schools, parks, and public transportation. They wanted access to those agencies supplying those services in a similar way that they wanted access to the police. That is, they wanted influence over both municipal and police services because evidently they were not providing public services up to the expectations of the respondents.

SAFETY

When participants were asked how safe it was to live in their community as compared to the proceeding year, 21 (15%) reported it was either very unsafe or unsafe, and 67 (46%) said nothing changed. Also, almost one in four reported their neighborhood was a safer place as compared to a year ago.

POLICE PERFORMANCE RATED

Based on the experience a participant had with Columbia police officers:

- 100 (69%) rated police performance as professional
- 13 (9%) rated police performance as fair
- 19 (13%) rated police performance as frightening
- 14 (10%) missing

Also, when survey takers reported on the performance of officers at crime or accident scenes, 68 (47%) said response time was good or excellent, 70 (48%) said officers solved the problem, 77 (53%) said officers put them at ease, 76 (52%) said officers were helpful, and 98 (67%) said officers were dressed appropriately.

POLICE EFFECTIVENESS

When participants were asked how effective the department was in responding to neighborhood problems, findings from the survey revealed the police department was:

- Effective or very effective: 78 (54%)
- Ineffective: 51 (35%)
- Didn't know: 8 (6%)
- Thought police had their own agenda: 9 (6%)

What else did the respondents think? Consistent with the findings from the other jurisdictions, most of the participants thought that specific officers should spend more time making personal contact with neighborhood residents, they should be assigned to a neighborhood on a long-term basis, and that they should be more involved with school activities. Also, 30 (21%) thought police talked down to them, but many said officers listened to the neighborhood's non-criminal concerns. Also, almost one-half of the residents in this investigation said they were comfortable in taking their suggestions or complaints to the police, and most felt that making the community safer should be a joint effort between the police and the people who lived there.

THE FUTURE

When they were asked about the future safety of their neighborhood, the following information was learned:

- A better place to live: 15 (10%)
- Will stay about the same: 44 (30%)
- A worse place to live: 45 (31%)
- Not sure about the future: 42 (29%)

It appears that the survey takers were divided in their responses. The many "not sure" reports could easily sway the outcome of those answers.

SUMMARY

A brief history of Columbia, South Carolina was offered, including demographics. The catalysts behind community policing in Columbia were characterized as crime rates, police leadership, church leadership, Federal Comprehensive Communities Program, and the initiatives taken by the individuals residing in the neighborhoods. Conclusions drawn by community policing observers suggest that Columbia appears to be committed to providing quality police service through conceptual community policing initiatives. The findings offered through a study gave evidence to aid in a better understanding of how some community members saw police outreach and their own neighborhood circumstances. Gangs and juveniles, street drug activity, and home invasion were seen as their most serious neighborhood problems. Remedies did not seem to match those problems in the sense that municipal services were of greater concern than police services. Municipal services that were problematic for the participants consisted of health care, public transportation, and public schools—specifically quality teachers. Safety issues continued to be of concern to the participants in that little had changed over the year for them, yet most of the participants rated officer performance as professional. Nonetheless, most felt unsafe in the community and the future didn't look any brighter.

CONCLUSION: COLUMBIA, SOUTH CAROLINA

Based on evidence provided by 146 residents of Columbia and public records of both the city of Columbia and the Columbia Police Department, crime is not under control in their neighborhoods, fear of crime levels had not changed and are believed to be high among the survey takers, and quality of life experiences seem suspect. One implication arising from these findings is that the community tends to be less orderly than expected (southern politeness) and the largest part of their disorder has to do with inadequate city or municipal services such as inadequate education in public schools, a lack of knowledge and information shared among community members, and a lack of predictability or stability concerning city and police services. These uncertainties impact life experiences and life chances of some individuals living in those communities.

That is, regardless of what the police department does to advance the safety of the citizens of Columbia, when other city services are inadequate, arresting bad guys has less to do with life experiences than expected.

The rationale for this thought is linked to the findings. That is, when competent individuals talk about basic needs such as health care and public transportation, when they possess little knowledge of the justice system, have family members and friends locked up,[13] and are suspicious of police supervision concerning their own children, then how can the findings be interpreted? For instance, it was reported that gangs and youth and home invasion topped their list of serious neighborhood problems, but their reported remedies did not take the form of cracking down on youths or controlling the streets but rather, provided transportation to visit a health clinic. The community gives lip service to the CPD, in return, police provide an official agenda that misses the mark. Each side fails to understand that it takes more than a professional police department, which the Columbia Police Department appears to be, to provide services that control crime, reduce the fear of crime, and enhance the life experiences of its constituents. However, individual police workers were highly respected and from the evidence, it appeared they worked hard toward helping community members; official policy was another matter.

The central question of this collective study was: does police practice enhance neighborhood safety issues and provide social order or stability? It was believed that community police strategies give rise to crime control, reductions in the fear of crime, and enhancements in resident quality of life experiences. It was assumed that if community members, especially culturally diverse members, influenced the decisions of the police, it would be more likely that public safety and lifestyle experiences would be enhanced.

There appears to be support for community members to attend community meetings, but they do not engage in a police or, more importantly, municipal decision-making process. Compelling evidence indicates that the primary question investigated was not supported.

One way to better understand the outcomes in Columbia might be to consider that groups always engage in a struggle over resources. The group with the most resources wins in that struggle, and exploits the losers. This perspective is known as conflict theory. It would appear that police and municipal agencies, or more specifically those who control municipal policy, hold more resources than community members, and consequently, policy makers win in the struggle. How are community members exploited? As we look at the various levels of reality other than those given in the official documents and Websites of Columbia, we tend to follow a logical imperative to unmask pretensions.[14] Although it might not be their intention, the police linked with the church in Columbia can damn souls and imprison bodies at the same time. Also, the police encourage community meetings, and attend them, but empowerment is more than meetings. In total, keeping people ignorant has benefits. This thought is congruent with writers who advocate that it is better to be conscious than unconscious and that consciousness is a condition of freedom.[15] The public agencies seem to supply fewer services than needed, suggesting the once-inferior education is linked to a fear of crime and a fear of police. Despite both municipal and police services, lifestyle experiences remain at unreasonable levels. However, would those who live at unreasonable levels really know how unreasonable they are?

For instance, there is a suspicion that a number of participants have little knowledge about the justice system, city services, and social services in Columbia. They knew little about how public agencies operate, such as health care and education. Even if many of the participants were empowered to influence police and city decision-making policies, how can people make an informed decision about municipal solutions when they don't understand how it works or who to call for hygiene care? An even larger thought is that:

> If those individuals involved with community meetings, council meetings, and the police have little real knowledge or control of police and city services, then how much knowledge or control do individuals have who don't attend community meetings?

One suggestion[16] is that Columbia's Council of Neighborhoods (CCN) as a community-based umbrella organization should coordinate more than the activities of neighborhood organizations. Perhaps this organization could reach out to those residents who do not attend meetings. Knowledge and training should become part of their outreach. They could coordinate a training program in collaboration with public agencies and the local community colleges. The community colleges of Columbia could provide "applied" curriculum[17] with a focus on how to deal with public agencies, instructional guidance, classrooms, and classroom equipment (overheads and so on). The public agencies could provide information and instructors. Residents could attend courses co-instructed by public agency personnel (including the police) with guidance from community college personnel. However, one concern is that the CCN is self-contained as is each group linked to it, and they define their own community boundaries and mission. What happens to those individuals who are not joiners, meeting goers, or who are too young, too old, too challenged, or those who work all the time? Is the CCN in a position to exclude members and does that exclusion deny certain members their constitutional guarantees? The people of Columbia and the public agencies through their managers and constituents have done an excellent job to date but there are challenges in the 21st century which seem to relate to community—all people in the community and how to advance them.

ENDNOTES

1. For a complete report see Ferguson, C. U. (2002). Creative community policing initiatives in Columbia, South Carolina. In Dennis J. Stevens (Ed.), *Communities and policing*, (pp. 45–76). Upper Saddle River, NJ: Prentice Hall. Carroy Ferguson is available at: carroy.ferguson @umb.edu. And Kelling, G. (1998). Columbia's Comprehensive Communities Program: A Case Study. Provided by the Columbia, South Carolina Police Department from their archives. However, this chapter would not have been possible without the help of Richard Hines of the Columbia, South Carolina Police Department who provided much of the groundwork and information. Richard Hines is available at: scpdrhines@columbiasc.net or (803)733-8411.

2. See http://www.census.gov.

3. The average home in 1999 was valued at approximately $83,000, and the median income of the population was $23,200. Approximately 20 percent of all families in Columbia live below the poverty line, while 30 percent of African Americans live below the poverty line. About 45 percent of the population own their own homes, as compared to a national average of 65 percent.

4. The Lead Organizations & Partners are: City of Columbia Neighborhood and Community Associations; City of Columbia Police Department; Richland County School District One; Carolina Peace Resource Center; Downtown Columbia Merchants' Association; Five Points Merchants Association; Community Service Organizations; City of Columbia Division/ Departments; State Criminal Justice Agencies; General Sessions Court; South Carolina Fifth

Circuit; Solicitor's Office; and the U.S. Attorney's Office.

5. See Ferguson, 2002 and Kelling, 1998.

6. See Ferguson, 2002, p. 49.

7. See Kelling, 1998, p. 25.

8. CCN's Website can be found at http://www.columbiasc.net/city/.

9. All of the above commentary can be found on the CCN Website at http://www.columbiasc.net/city/counofn.htm.

10. BOTEC Analysis Corporation, 1998; CCN, 2001; CPD, 2001; Ferguson, 2002; Heinz & Manikas, 1992; Kelling, 1998. The following are strengths the help pull community policing together in Columbia according to those authors.

1. the chief of police is highly respected and enjoys local political, social, and media support for his community policing vision

2. Columbia's neighborhoods are well-organized both internally and among themselves, through the Columbia Council of Neighborhoods

3. churches have maintained and expanded their presence in Columbia's inner city neighborhoods, playing an active role in its reconstruction

4. there is a level of coordination and cooperation among city agencies, especially among police, housing, planning, and school departments, as exemplified by the City's Planning Department being the administrative body for Columbia's CCP effort, the

Police Department as the lead agency, and the Columbia Council of Neighborhoods being an overarching community agency in the City's community policing initiatives

5. the city's size seems to make many of its problems manageable in terms of a community policing philosophy and strategy

6. Columbia's community policing initiatives seem to have established a common vision for community policing among police and community leaders, bureaucrats, and citizens

11. Those areas included deployment of routine police auto, bike, and boat patrol, decisions on mini stations, building owner notification, use of police force, priorities of calls for service, police officer disciplinary actions, police training, and officer promotions.

12. Jail and prison visits was not an isolated response. One thought is that as many as 30 (21%) of the respondents had family members and friends in jail or prison. Considering the age of the average participant, more than likely the individual in jail was a son, brother, father, or daughter.

13. The Department of Corrections in South Carolina supervises over 40,000 individuals, in a state with approximately 3.1 million residents (which is similar to the population of the entire city of Chicago). It would seem that many people living in South Carolina, especially blacks, are in prison, just got out of prison, or someone they know or love is in the process. Of interest, of those incarcerated, 69% are black, and 30% are white. In 2000, 23% of all new prison admissions were for dangerous drugs. Source: http://www.bop.gov/.

14. See Berger, P. L. (1963). *Invitation to sociology: A humanistic perspective* (p. 38). Garden City, NJ: Anchor Books.

15. Ibid. p. 175.

16. Yes! It is easy to make recommendations when you're 900 miles away. But it is a similar suggestion for cities throughout the United States where constituents—all constituents— need to step up and become responsible for community outcomes. However, since most constituents have little knowledge of public agencies, they need to learn. It's probably less expensive and more efficient to train constituents than to supply poor service.

17. Applied means to pull together a collection of currently operating public agencies, and perhaps have agency personnel co-instruct courses or sit on panels. Mission: explaining how to deal with those agencies; phone numbers, forms, benefits, services provided, and process. For instance, how to get a pothole filled by the Department of Streets or how to board a vacant building or how to have a business license revoked. The community colleges would help residents to advance themselves through non-degreed, no cost programs (the state can financially support some of the actual costs such as payroll to college personnel who participate at different levels), the agencies would learn about the communities they serve (and it's a great source of personnel). Of course, the ultimate goal and benefit is that public agencies would become democratic in their process, and the police as facilitators would move closer to their mission of public safety.

CHAPTER 6

TESTING POLICE PERFORMANCE IN COLUMBUS, OHIO

INTRODUCTION

In many ways, Columbus typifies America's larger cities, but it lacks the notoriety of cities such as San Antonio and the international flavor of cities such as Boston. Therefore, its value to investigators of police strategies might prove resourceful as a community police model. The Columbus Division of Police (CDP) in Columbus, Ohio[1] services 711,470 individuals living in 212 square miles.[2] Of that population, 483,332 (68%) are white, 174,065 (25%) are black, 24,495 (3%) are Asian, and 17,471 (3%) are Latino. There are approximately 1,800 sworn officers employed by the CDP which is an equivalent of 2.6 sworn officers per each 1,000 residents.[3] Columbus is one of the fastest growing cities in the Midwest, and its downtown is evidence of its energy and distinguished character. It is the home of Ohio State University, and it is the state capital of Ohio.

Chief James G. Jackson said that community police and problem oriented policing "are often described as solutions to traditional policing strategies, and have become buzzwords and/or icons in many police and academic circles. The ideals of policing in collaboration with the community and policing to solve problems are sound principles that can hold promise for increasing the effectiveness of police agencies like the CDP."[4] Yet, the CDP learned the hard way. Although, the CDP was successful in meeting many of their goals, it was not without fault and the current threat of federal litigation against the CDP has yet to be resolved.[5]

EARLY EXPERIENCES OF THE CDP

What the CDP experienced in the last decade was that most efforts by police agencies to become community oriented were programs or "smoke screens" (walking patrols, bicycle patrols, police cars, police stations, and Websites decorated with a community police emblem) intended to improve relations or resolve hostility between residents and the police. While those practices are helpful to their understanding of community police strategies, they do not result in a long-term philosophical change in the way a police organization conducts business. In the last years of the 20th century, the CDP realized that when an agency wants to reduce the fear of crime and crime itself and enhance the quality of life standards for community members, piece-mealing a community police program was neither efficient nor effective. Unfortunately, the CDP learned community police skills the hard way. During their early period of transformation from an agency centered in a reactive response versus a proactive response, the CDP learned that:

1. Community oriented policing initiatives are generally characterized by unclear objectives and lack of a shared vision among police personnel (including command officers), community members, and civic leaders
2. Community police as a department-wide philosophy is rarely practiced by any police agency
3. Many police agencies practice a form of community police initiatives, but few understand its major concepts

Some experiences that brought them to those conclusions included a survey they conducted in 1994 with residents in Columbus. The CDP wanted to know what others thought about their police services. In general, residents reported they wanted police services tailored to individual community needs, a better resolution of crime and safety problems, more police presence, greater input to and communication with the police department, increased enforcement of quality of life violations, and closer relationships with the officers working in the neighborhoods. To meet those aims, police leadership developed the Mission Aligned Policing Philosophy and the Strategic Response Bureau to conduct strategy.

The Strategic Response Bureau (SRB), with a staff of nearly one hundred officers and supervisors, was created to better identify problems related to the police mission and develop creative solutions to impact them. The difficulty came in getting officers to break the mold of reactive responses and learn to solve problems that they faced creatively and collaboratively. The bureau's primary function was problem solving.

IMPLEMENTING PROBLEM SOLVING

To accomplish a transition from a crime-fighting agency to a problem solving one, the CPD focused on four activities:

1. Taught problem solving skills to officers
2. Collected, analyzed, and disseminated crime statistics

3. Group discussions with officers about "best solutions"
4. Officers' activities were monitored

Through skill development, application, and feedback community officers learned to be proficient problem solvers.

RESISTANCE TO CHANGE

The change to a community police program was publicized and poised to be an immediate success story. The first two years that followed the notoriety were rife with struggles, frustrations, and unexpected circumstances. Bridges (1991) described what he called "The Neutral Zone," a "very difficult time" when command becomes impatient and asks, "How long is it going to take you to implement those changes?" In retrospect, "The Neutral Zone" seemed to be one of the experiences of men and women of the CDP, too. Top command wanted quantifiable results and put pressure on the SRB to demonstrate success. Meanwhile, members of the new operation felt the pressure to produce, yet found they were unable to follow their own plans of operation. The principal planners at the SRB were unable to successfully implement the program. Many questioned the plan itself and the ability of those involved to conduct it. Little did they know that what they were experiencing was a normal part of a process of change. What the CDP experienced was the unpleasant period of transition known as the neutral zone. Bridges lists six steps to take to survive the neutral zone. These include:

1. Protecting people from further changes
2. Reviewing policies and procedures
3. Examining relationships and organizational structure
4. Setting short range goals
5. Promising obtainable goals
6. Helping supervisors and managers learn what they need to function successfully

The time in the neutral zone can actually be a creative period if appropriate action is taken. Without the benefit of Bridge's advice, members of SRB eventually discovered these steps for themselves. Policies and procedures were evaluated and changed with input of workers, supervisors, and community members. Unproductive reporting relationships were changed and the organizational structure modified to make communications easier and maximize the ability of the various components to accomplish their tasks and collaborate with other units. It should be noted that almost from the beginning of the new initiative at the CDP, outside, independent evaluation was conducted by the Ohio State University Criminal Justice Research Center, under the direction of Professor C. Ronald Huff.[6]

DEPARTMENT OF JUSTICE INVESTIGATION

In addition to some police personnel resistance to a change in the method of police service through community police efforts, the CDP experienced other situations that seemed to complicate police efforts. That is, the US Department of Justice (DOJ) initiated an investigation of the department for alleged misconduct of police officers.

Specifically, a former and apparently disgruntled police officer who quit the department to avoid being fired went to DOJ alleging violations of citizens' rights regarding use of force in Columbus. He provided a few names of potential victims. The DOJ conducted a preliminary investigation. They came to Columbus to meet with officials and information provided indicated that they informed Columbus officials that they did not foresee a major investigation but wanted to follow-up on the information they had been presented by the former officer.

Coincidentally, this investigation occurred during the same time period when the Columbus city administration attempted to redirect police services since they were unhappy with the results from community police efforts. There are indicators that some city officials may have encouraged the DOJ to conduct a full investigation as they felt it might lead to the Chief's dismissal. DOJ was given additional names, mostly of people who had filed complaints alleging excessive or unnecessary use of force. It appears that DOJ investigators did not interview any of the police personnel involved in those situations, only the alleged victims. They did, however, review official police documentation. DOJ eventually asked the city to enter into a consent decree that would require intervention and oversight of CPD.

The Fraternal Order of Police (FOP) intervened and was named a party to the case. DOJ, the City, and the FOP tried to negotiate but talks broke down and DOJ filed suit in Federal District Court. The judge in the case reviewed it and told the parties to go back into negotiations. Not much has happened since that time but at a conference in Chicago, the DOJ Lead Investigators in the Columbus case spoke. They gave the impression (according to a CPD/FOP person in the audience) that they would like to find a way to get out of the case.

The long and short of it is there may be a few isolated cases of improper conduct but nothing close to the "pattern and practice" of abuse alleged by certain officers. There may have been some motivation on the part of some former city administration officials to use the DOJ investigation to accomplish their goal of getting rid of the chief. The case was still pending in the summer of 2001 and there is no indication at this point of when and how it will be resolved.

CRIME REPORT

In reviewing a 9-year crime report, there appears to be no marked improvement in crime in Columbus, Ohio (see Table 6.1). That is, despite minor changes in the

TABLE 6.1 **Uniform Crime Index Offenses* Nine Year Comparison**

CRIME	1990	1991	1992	1993	1994	1995	1996	1997	1998
Murder	92	139	113	105	100	78	90	83	79
Rape	647	651	685	658	679	636	571	696	668
Robbery	3,541	3,747	3,595	3,887	3,599	3,330	3,318	3,104	2,615
Aggravated Assault	2,735	2,686	2,859	2,496	2,383	2,582	2,238	2,103	2,040
Burglary	14,982	16,398	15,064	13,055	13,088	13,146	13,013	13,453	13,526
Theft/Larceny	32,387	32,989	31,051	29,051	29,776	31,905	34,244	35,882	36,338
Vehicle Theft	8,466	8,874	7,136	7,070	6,720	7,038	7,610	7,118	7,343
Arson	926	875	995	1,029	1,035	915	808	778	813
Total	63,622	66,359	60,503	57,351	57,378	59,630	61,892	63,217	63,422
Population	632,910	638,533	643,028	646,933	647,860	657,487	657,045	696,849	696,849
Rate Per 1,000 Population	100.7	103.9	94.1	88.7	88.6	90.7	91.7	90.7	91.0

Source: The Columbus Division of Police.

population base, the crime rate per 1,000 population has been consistently around 90 for the past four years and at 88 for the two preceding years. However, from 1990 and 1991, there appears to be a decline in those crimes measured. Therefore, it could be argued that the crime rate has not necessarily reflected a significant change in the past six years. However, as we review crime in 1999 (see Table 6.2), it appears that crimes of violence are on the rise.

■ ■ ■ ■ ■

CHIEF JAMES G. JACKSON TALKS ABOUT COMMUNITY POLICING

It is my pleasure to share with you some of the benefits I believe the Columbus, Ohio Division of Police has enjoyed regarding our commitment to Community Policing. The process for developing the Division's commitment to the COP philosophy, and the corresponding process for implementing the mechanics is both time consuming, and often problematic. Changing attitudes and responses in the policing business requires patience and persistence. However, it seems this is the direction we in law enforcement should be going, and more importantly, it appears this approach will prove to be (long-term) effective and efficient.

Community police with the Columbus Division of Police probably began, as it did with most agencies, with our old Crime Prevention Unit. While very popular with the

continued

Continued

community groups it trained and interacted with, and effective as far as it could be within its limited scope and range, most community members were not dramatically impacted by its efforts.

Our fairly recent commitment to the COP process via the creation of the Strategic Response Bureau has provided our Division and the community with a fresh approach to addressing community problems and concerns. With the inclusion of a number of service units under one umbrella bureau, our goal is to permit a comprehensive approach to dealing with often endemic and long-standing challenges. Additionally, other Division resources including traditional patrol officers, community resource officers, bike patrol officers, and walking officers supported by other Division (and outside resources) all help to round out our ability to assist our community members.

Not surprisingly, in-house responses to non-traditional, proactive and problem-solving oriented strategies have been mixed, however, it is my belief that with both officers and community members alike seeing improving results from community responsive policing, there will ultimately be greater general support for our efforts. In conclusion, there is little question that COP is the philosophy for law enforcement agencies of the future. The challenges are many and sometimes difficult to overcome, however, with persistence and commitment, the challenges facing COP will prove to be the stepping stones to success. You have my best wishes for your continued and future success.

James G. Jackson, Chief of Police, 12/6/99

TABLE 6.2   1999

OFFENSE	TOTALS
Murder/Manslaughter	113
Rape	650
Robbery	3,026
Aggravated Assault	2,046
Burglary	14,070
Larceny over $500.00	8,919
Larceny under $500.00	25,740
Vehicle Theft	7,277
Other Assaults	19,306
Forgery	2,268
Fraud/Embezzlement	1,906
Indecent Exposure	150
Molestation	249
Other Sex Crimes	193
All Other	19,585

AN EVALUATION OF CDP'S COP/POP EFFORTS[7]

The CDP distributed a survey between September 1998 and August 1999 to evaluate community police efforts. What was measured was the COP/POP attitudes of three groups: 40 CDP uniformed patrol officers who had little direct contact with COP/POP initiatives, 70 community members in Columbus who had direct contract with those initiatives, and 36 commanders and related personnel in police departments primarily throughout the state of Ohio. Their test was conducted two years after CDP established its COP/POP initiatives in Columbus.

SURVEY 1: CDP PATROL OFFICERS

When the data of the patrol officers were polled, distinctive patterns arose. For example, the following typical response from a patrol officer typified the reports of majority of the patrol officers concerning the Community Liaison Officers (CLOs). They "have the hardest job (on the CDP by) dealing with the public and police." Furthermore, "Liaison officers (have) access to people and (patrol) officers to answers to questions." Liaison officers "help explain what patrol is really all about."

Statistical evidence supported the above comments in that over one-half of the patrol officers reported that they felt confident about the SRB and the bureau's liaison officers specifically assigned to interact with community members, community organizations, and CDP personnel such as the patrol officers themselves. Evidently, patrol officers saw the SRB and CLOs as assets to both the community and the department.

SURVEY 2: COMMUNITY MEMBERS

Specifically, there were several remarks that seemed to typify the primary issues addressed by the community member respondents. For instance, the efforts of the community police liaison officers were typified in the respondent who stated that "the liaison officer in our community has been very effective and supportive of our concerns." Another respondent added, "He comes to all meetings and is well respected for his response to our needs." Accordingly, the statistical results were no surprise when 95% (67) of the respondents reported that COP was a change for the better for Columbus, yet only 48% (34) felt that CDP was doing all it should be regarding COP. Seventy-two percent (50) of the community members polled reported the CDP was effective in solving crime in their neighborhood and 76% (53) felt that police effectiveness had improved since the inception of COP. When asked specifically about the SRB and the COP Program, most of the respondents were aware of the program and 87% (61) felt the program improved police service. Regarding the Community Liaison Officers (CLOs), almost all of the participants reported that Liaison Officers provided assistance in problem solving, that better information was available due to those officers, and 91% (64) felt that the officers were an improvement in providing police services.

SURVEY 3: OTHER POLICE AGENCIES

Of 36 similar sized police agencies, 88% (32) of their commanders endorsed COP and most reported similar experiences as CDP.

SURVEY CONCLUSION

The CDP reported that they had strengthened its relationship with the community, involved citizens in efforts to address crime and safety problems, and enhanced its ability to effectively police the City of Columbus. The Division was become a high-performance police organization, focused on not only increasing effectiveness in dealing with crime and safety problems, but also on fostering ongoing learning, encouraging innovation, and maximizing the use of information technology to improve law enforcement. Did future investigators find similar results?

TESTING POLICE PERFORMANCE
IN COLUMBUS, OHIO

There were 181 surveys completed by residents of Columbus, Ohio. They lived in Columbus for an average of 14 years and the typical survey taker was 45 years of age (see Table 6.3). Thirty-three (18%) of them characterized their employment as a blue-collar job, and 37 (20%) as a white-collar job. Also, 14 (8%) were retired, 15 (8%) were students, and 24 (13%) reported they worked in the retail business. Finally, 25 (14%) reported they were business owners, but 33 (18%) participants left this question unanswered, were unemployed, or were between jobs.

There were 61 (33%) females and 119 (66%) males. One hundred twenty-eight (71%) described themselves as white, 6 (3%) as black, 12 (7%) as Latino, 20 (11%) as Asian, and 15 (8%) left this question blank.

When they were asked what homeland they identified with the most often, 147 (81%) reported it was the USA, 15 (8%) said Western Europe, and 9 (5%) said Haiti, the Dominican Republic, and/or the Caribbean. Five (3%) reported Central or South America or Mexico, and another 5 (3%) said China or Asia.

Concerning languages spoken at home, 120 (66%) spoke only English, 46 (25%) spoke English and another language. None spoke only Spanish or Portuguese at home. Finally, 131 (72%) of the respondents rented and 32 (18%) owned their home.

TABLE 6.3   Characteristics of Columbus, Ohio Sample, N = 181

	NUMBERS	PERCENTS[*]/RANGE
Length of Time	14 years	0–42 years
Age	45	21–72
Occupation		
Blue Collar	33	18%
White Collar	37	20%
Retired	14	8%
Student	15	8%
Retail	24	13%
Business Owner	25	14%
Other/Missing	33	18%
Gender		
Females	61	34%
Males	119	66%
Race		
White	128	71%
Black	6	3%
Latino	12	7%
Asian	20	11%
Missing	15	8%
Homeland		
Western Europe	15	8%
Eastern Europe	0	0%
Haiti/Dominican/Caribbean	9	5%
Central/South America/Mexico	5	3%
Cape Verde/Cuba	0	0%
China/Asia	5	3%
USA	147	81%
Language Spoken Home		
English	120	66%
English and another language	46	25%
Only Spanish or Portuguese	0	0%
Other/Missing	15	8%
Residents		
Rented	131	72%
Owned	32	18%
Lived with others	18	10%

[*]All percents rounded. Missing cases not always included.

MAKING DECISIONS AND MEETINGS

Rarely did they report involvement in any of the decision-making processes conducted by the police. Yet, 156 (86%) reported they would participate in police discussions, if asked.

At community meetings, 145 (80%) reported that sometimes or very often community members worked together, but 35 (19%) said they seldom worked together at meetings. Although, 162 (90%) participants reported neighborhood people were often encouraged to attend community police meetings often. Yet, six of every ten reported only sometimes or seldom had they received a to-do list as a result of those meetings. Also, during those encounters or meetings, 116 (64%) said they were rarely encouraged to develop their own problem solving remedies. At many meetings, 113 (62%) participants revealed police monopolized those conversations with enforcement discussions, but less than often they were previous problem solving plans changed to fit new findings. Yet, 112 (62%) respondents said they were sure the solutions coming from problem solving discussions were practical. But, 69 (38%) reported solutions of the officers were impractical or they weren't sure.

CHANGES

When Columbus residents were asked in what way their community was safer since the community started meetings (as opposed to the participant attending meetings), many comments were offered which fit the following categories:

- Response time of officers was about the same: 12 (7%)
- Officers now identified with the neighborhood: 43 (24%)
- People who previously remained quiet about crime now talked about it: 97 (54%)
- Didn't know or offered no comment: 29 (16%)

And, 30 (17%) reported police were more visible, while 114 (63%) reported that one of the ways police contributed to their safety was that residents felt a sense of identity or a sense of belonging to the neighborhood.

GREATEST NEIGHBORHOOD PROBLEMS

The 181 Columbus residents reported their most serious neighborhood issues were:

- Home invasion
- Street drug activity
- Streets, lights, empty buildings, and graffiti

- Fear or lack of trust of police
- Gangs and juveniles
- Parking, traffic, and speeders
- Panhandlers and prostitutes

Specifically, 60 (33%) reported their greatest neighborhood problem was home invasion, and 33 (18%) reported it was street drug activity. A tie existed in third place between streets, lights, empty buildings, and graffiti and a fear or lack of trust of police, reported 27 (15%) residents respectively. Fourteen (8%) participants reported it was gangs and juveniles, and another 14 (8%) reported it was parking, traffic, and speeders. Finally, 6 (4%) participants reported it was either panhandlers and prostitutes or "other."

REMEDIES

When Columbus residents were asked what should be done to curb neighborhood problems, the majority of them described the following conceptual categories:

- Quality policing and municipal services
- Youth and gang supervision

One hundred and twenty-three (68%) residents said the best way to curb their most serious community problems was through quality policing and municipal services. That is, enforcement and city services were equally sought as remedies to community problems. Police service included primarily honest communication with neighborhoods and consistent enforcement of laws. The people polled revealed that they wanted to know what crime and related events happened in their neighborhoods (as opposed to knowing what was happening in the entire police department) and they wanted everyone treated "fairly" which should not be construed as "equally." They made an effort to describe differences between fairly and equally. Fairly meant that since they were law-abiding residents, they should receive more respect from the police department and, as a result, quality municipal services (although police service was implied, it came in second to services provided by the city of Columbus). That is, they should receive the bulk of city services and other Columbus residents—"especially," one resident typified, "more than those lazy welfare people who get everything for free." The few thoughts that related to how home invasion could be controlled included more auto, biking, and walking patrols.

The residents wanted more city services, including holiday parades in their neighborhoods instead of elsewhere in the city, more control over social services (they saw state as city services), and more control over building, street, and park departments in Columbus. Several mentioned that it was unfair to have community correctional facilities and halfway houses in their community. They wanted those facilities placed in the "bad parts of town where animals like them lived, not here," one resident wrote.

Community members revealed two conceptual central themes:

- Police and city oversight committees
- Police and other city departments work together

Of all the residents in the Columbus investigation, 85 (47%) implied the way to solve serious neighborhood problems was through their empowered participation on police and city oversight committees. One influencing factor moving residents toward this conceptual category might be consistent with those 66 (36%) respondents who reported Columbus officers seldom, if ever, made them feel comfortable.

The residents made little distinction between law enforcement services and city amenities including street repairs, street light replacement (they wanted taller and brighter street lights), tree removal, abandoned buildings demolition, conversion of unused schools and city buildings into affordable housing (not welfare housing), better equipment for fire fighters, and greater cooperation between police and city services. One common thread in their answers was their lack of information. They wanted city and police information about city events, city service procedures, and outcomes. And, they wanted input into committees that developed plans and provided services. Finally, they wanted police service and city service to work under a similar direction and part of that direction included community influence and preferences; but that in itself was not their final answer. It appeared that influence over city committees was their first aim for the purpose of enhancing their quality of life experiences. Their second aim had to do with uniting policing and city services, but unlike the Boston respondents, they didn't want the police in control of city services. That is, 53 (29%) participants wanted city police and city service to work as one unit toward the common good.

SAFETY

When asked how safe it was to live in their community as compared to a year ago, 40 (22%) reported it was very unsafe, and 103 (57%) said nothing had changed. Twenty-one (12%) reported it was safer in their neighborhood as compared to last year, in fact, 15 (8%) said it was much safer.

POLICE PERFORMANCE RATED

Based on the experience a participant had with police:

- 115 (64%) rated police performance as professional
- 21 (12%) rated police performance as fair

- 44 (24%) rated police performance as intimidating
- 1 (1%) missing

Also, when survey takers talked about the performance of officers at a crime or an accident scene, 82 (45%) said response time was good or excellent, 84 (46%) said officers solved the problem, and 87 (48%) said officers put them at ease. Also, 95 (52%) participants said officers were helpful, and 110 (61%) said officers were dressed appropriately.

POLICE EFFECTIVENESS

When participants were asked how effective the department was in responding to neighborhood problems, findings revealed the police department was:

- Effective or very effective: 129 (71%)
- Ineffective: 102 (56%)
- Police had their own agenda: 1 (.6%)

What else did respondents think? Almost all thought specific officers should spend more time making personal contact with neighborhood residents, they should be responsible for a neighborhood on a long-term basis, and they should be more involved with school activities. Also, 99 (47%) revealed police generally talked down to them, however, some thought police listened to their non-criminal concerns. However, 127 (60%) survey takers reported they were comfortable in taking their suggestions or complaints to police, and most felt that making the community safe should be a joint effort between police and community.

THE FUTURE

When asked about the future of their community's safety, they said:

- It would be better place to live: 15 (8%)
- It will stay about the same: 21 (12%)
- It will become a worse place to live: 103 (57%)
- Not sure: 40 (22%)

SUMMARY

Although participant age and residence time is consistent with the larger sample, other characteristics are inconsistent. For instance, there were many more males than females. Also, race, homeland, and languages spoken showed less diversification than the sample at-large. Many thought community members helped police toward a safer environment, and the police and the community members felt a sense of identification with the neighborhood as a result of community meetings. The sample said home invasion, street drug activity, and streets, lights, empty buildings, and graffiti were among their most serious neighborhood problems. The way to solve their most serious community problems included greater municipal services and police patrols. They wanted to know more about events in their neighborhoods and wanted a form of control over police and municipal oversight committees. They wanted police and city services unified, and wanted fewer city amenities given to welfare recipients. Over three-fourths of the sample thought that Columbus was either unsafe or had not changed in the past year, although they rated individual police performance as very professional along with their police department's effectiveness. However, many participants anticipated their neighborhood becoming a worse place to live in the future.

CONCLUSION: COLUMBUS, OHIO

Based on evidence provided by 181 Columbus residents, public records of the city of Columbus, and public records of the Columbus Division of Police, the fear of crime was pervasive and greater when this investigation was conducted than in the previous year and their standards of life experiences were compromised. Furthermore, residents were not optimistic about their future even though officer conduct was rated as professional and the police department was rated as highly effective. Also, they felt many of the city's resources were distributed to undeserving citizens of Columbus. Therefore, it would be safe to argue, due in part to their fear of crime and loss of city services to individuals they thought were less productive, that many residents were not living at their expected lifestyle levels. Therefore, to answer the primary question under investigation: does police practice enhance neighborhood safety issues and provide social order or stability? It was believed prior to the investigation that community police strategies gave rise to crime control, reduced the fear of crime, and enhanced resident quality of life experiences. After the investigation, it was learned that while many attended meetings, there was little evidence that any one of them influenced police decision-making processes. One question arising from this finding is that if these residents didn't influence police policy, who did? Therefore there was little support for the idea that community members—regardless of their cultural diversity—influenced police decisions. Accordingly, public order was not necessarily enhanced through policing strategies. One remedy demanded by the residents of Columbus (or at least by those surveyed) was control over all city services to alter what they saw as an injustice.

There was a consensus on ways to solve serious neighborhood problems as compared to what those problems were in the community. The sample said they should receive most of the city services and that other residents of the city were not entitled to similar services. In part, as a result of meeting with other community members, six of ten respondents thought they should get more of what the city offers than others. They wanted "fairness" practiced, but fairness and equality were two different concepts for these residents.

One recommendation to enhance community "fairness" concepts might be to focus on elements that reduce resentment among groups such as confiding in community members as a group and utilizing their ideas to enhance their communities. Equally important, move problem-solving responsibilities to the communities. That is, community groups share with each other, in concert with city services (including the police), the development and performance of problem-solving tasks across the city. As groups work together, an understanding can develop and ultimately, through that understanding, hostility between groups can be reduced.

ENDNOTES

1. The Columbus Division of Police can be found on their Website at http://www.police.ci.columbus.oh.us/.

2. Source: US Census, 2000. [On-line]: Available at http://www.census.gov.

3. For a complete report see Stevens, D. J. (2001a). *Case studies in community policing* (pp. 91–120). Upper Saddle River, NJ: Prentice Hall.

4. Found on CDP's Website: http://www.police.ci.columbus.oh.us/.

5. As of August, 2001.

6. Professor Huff was president of the American Society of Criminologists in 2000–2001.

7. This study was conducted by Commander Kent Shafer of the SRB and his staff.

■ ■ ■ ■ ■

CHAPTER 7

TESTING POLICE PERFORMANCE IN MIAMI-DADE COUNTY, FLORIDA

MIAMI-DADE POLICE DEPARTMENT HISTORY

Dade County was established in 1836, and encompassed an area which presently consists of Dade, Broward, Palm Beach, and Martin Counties. In the early years, the area was policed by three deputies on horseback. Dade's county seat was moved from Juno to Miami in 1899, when the population of Miami was approximately 5,000. Prior to this time, Dade's sheriffs were appointed by the governor. From the turn of the century through 1966, the office of the sheriff was an elected position.

By 1950, Dade County's population had grown to 495,000, and the jurisdiction area had been reduced to approximately its present 2,139 square miles (5,540 square kilometers). The metropolitan form of government was approved in 1957, and the Dade County Sheriff's Office was subsequently renamed the Public Safety Department.

In 1960, in addition to providing countywide police services, responsibility was assumed for police operations at the Port of Miami and Miami International Airport. There existed a long-standing controversy over the selection/election procedure for choosing a county sheriff that was finally resolved by voter mandate. Subsequently, non-elected sheriffs were appointed by the County Manager as Director of the Public Safety Department and Sheriff of Metropolitan-Dade County. The organizational structure, as determined by the Metropolitan Charter, included responsibility for fire protection, the jail and stockade, civil defense, animal control, and motor vehicle inspection, in addition to police functions.

By 1973, however, the department was divested of ancillary responsibilities in order to concentrate entirely on police services. During the 1970s, great strides were made toward professionalizing the department through development of innovative community programs, standard operating procedures, rules and regulations, and departmental training programs. As the complexity of its challenges grew, the department expanded its size and skills to keep pace. In 1997, Dade County voters decided to rename the county Miami-Dade County and the sheriff's department was named the Miami-Dade Police Department. In 2000, there were 3,002 sworn officers and 1,735 civilians employed by the MDPD who provided service for almost 2.2 million individuals in the Miami-Dade area. The US Census reports that 1.2 million (57%) of the population in the county of Miami-Dade represent a Hispanic or Latino population, 427,140 (19%) a black or African American population, and a 30,537 (1.4%) Asian population.[1] The balance are white. The Miami-Dade Police Department (MDPD)[2] in Miami, Florida reports that their mission is to commit its resources in partnership with the community to:

- Promote a safe and secure environment, free from crime and the fear of crime
- Maintain order and provide for the safe and expeditious flow of traffic
- Practice core values of integrity, respect, and fairness

DIRECTOR CARLOS ALVAREZ'S STATEMENT

The Miami-Dade Police Department is an internationally accredited law enforcement agency committed to maintaining the highest standards of individual and organizational integrity, while providing the most progressive and professional service to our community. Through the efforts of our dedicated personnel, and continued citizen support, the Department employs the most innovative crime-fighting strategies and state-of-the-art technologies. This dynamic unity empowers us to meet the difficult policing challenges of our diverse, urban community.

Historically, the Department has worked closely with the community to develop approaches that address the priorities of our citizens. We strive to provide the most effective crime prevention techniques, the most aggressive investigative responses, and the most proactive intervention programs. For several years, we have enjoyed consistent reductions in crime, and in the past two years those reductions have been dramatic.

Recently, we encountered one of our most unusual challenges. At a time when our community is facing rapid growth and hosting record numbers of visitors, the Department was tasked with continuing to effect reductions in crime far exceeding the national averages. With tremendous support from Mayor Alex Penelas, the County Commission, led by Chairperson Gwen Margolis, and County Manager Merrett Stierheim, we have embarked upon new initiatives tailored to the needs of individual neighborhoods throughout our community.

The reduction of violent street crime, particularly robbery, remains the cornerstone of our overall strategy. Enforcement activities designed to attack robbery affect almost every other street crime. Our Robbery Intervention Detail (RID) has been expanded with additional personnel and increased work hours—and the results have been remarkable. Robberies have decreased 53 percent in the past 8 years and 36 percent in the past 2 years alone. The Tourist Oriented Police Program (TOP) provides a variety of tourist-related assistance services. The success of the program is reflected by a dramatic 92 percent reduction in tourist robberies since 1992.

Our Tactical Narcotics Team (TNT) is deployed into neighborhoods where street-level drugs are sold, paying special attention to areas plagued by continual violence. We have also focused on violent offenders and career criminals, including habitual juvenile offenders and gang members. Again, the results have been outstanding. Street violence has been reduced and we have experienced our fewest number of homicides since 1978.

In addition, we have established community partnerships that allow us to customize enforcement initiatives to meet the unique needs of specific neighborhoods. These initiatives address the most topical local problems including burglary, prostitution, auto theft, drug sales, truancy, and traffic congestion. The programs involve education and intervention as well as traditional enforcement. Our primary service population has grown 22 percent since 1993; however, these citizen-driven strategies have resulted in the lowest crime rates in more than two decades.

To ensure that our commanders remain personally accountable for identifying and resolving both crime and quality-of-life issues within their areas of responsibility, we have implemented an extremely successful COMSTAT program. We've made extraordinary progress in computerizing our evidence storage and analysis process, and recently created a new Crime Analysis System (CAS) which allows for a more sophisticated analysis of individual crimes and trends. Currently, a Crime Information Data Warehouse is being developed to secure the most timely and accurate reporting of crime statistics. We have also automated the process we use to monitor sexual predators. This system ensures that every citizen can be apprised of the whereabouts of these dangerous individuals, and of course, we have taken every step possible to confirm that all of our systems are Year 2000 compliant.

Our priorities are driven by the needs and direction of our citizens. Every departmental employee has undergone intense human diversity and ethics training. Following recent events, the Public Corruption Section was developed to investigate all manners of corruption throughout Miami-Dade County. In direct response to concerns from our residential neighborhoods, we have implemented an Environmental Crimes Investigative Unit to handle illegal dumping and improper disposal of industrial waste. We have expanded our Community Oriented Policing Squads (COPS) to every district, and worked closely with local businesses to build Community Work Stations in public areas throughout the county. To furnish the most comprehensive patrol coverage possible, we have joined forces with every municipal police agency, granting them countywide jurisdiction, so that regardless of duty status, every officer will always be available to assist our citizens. Additionally, we have begun construction of the Carol City District Station to meet area service demands.

As our officers are frequently the first to arrive at emergency situations, patrol vehicles are now equipped with Automated External Defibrillators. To ensure that our 911 emergency telephone number is always available, we have implemented an easily remembered, non-emergency telephone number—(305) 4-POLICE. These technological advancements give us greater opportunities to save lives.

We are committed to the youth of our community. We continue to place the highest priority on programs such as Drug Abuse Resistance Education (DARE), Police Athletic League (PAL), "Join a Team Not a Gang," Gang Resistance Education and Training (GREAT), and "Don't Let Alcohol Be Your Last Taste Of Life," which teach young people the dangers of substance abuse, negative peer pressure, and gang involvement. The Juvenile Assessment Center (JAC) processes arrested juveniles and provides the most effective diversionary programs immediately after arrest. This technique gives us the best opportunity to keep kids out of the criminal justice system. Since its opening in 1997, the JAC has provided this service to more than 31,000 young people.

Certainly, no community with more than two million residents can be completely crime free. However, this community has every right to be proud of the progress we have made since the late 1980s. Miami-Dade County is now safe for residents and visitors. We have developed a strong partnership between our citizens, elected officials, and law enforcement authorities to successfully attack one of the most intractable problems in modern society—the plague of violent crime.

We will continue to encounter new and difficult challenges. However, I am proud to report that we have already developed an effective model of community partnership. We have implemented innovative programs which have clearly and substantially reduced crime. We are confident that we will effectively meet the needs of the community we are so proud to serve.

CITIZENS CRIME WATCH
OF MIAMI-DADE COUNTY

In November 1974, an area in Southwest Dade County was plagued by rumors of a "Gentle Rapist." At that time there were no effective direct lines of communication between police and the people. In response to this problem, a concerned citizen called a meeting of her neighbors. She arranged to have the police officers assigned to the "Gentle Rapist" case speak to the group. The initial reaction was to form a vigilante group, however, the officers convinced them there was a more beneficial approach to their problem—a crime prevention group. The officers taught the group how to protect their families, their homes, and themselves. This meeting served as a model for the Neighborhood Watch program.

Encouraged by the interest of her neighbors, this caring citizen assembled a group representing a cross section of residents in Dade County. They formulated a plan to introduce the neighborhood watch concept throughout Dade County. The plan consisted of the citizens organizing the watch groups. The police provided information about the crimes in their respective neighborhoods. They initiated training in crime prevention. The first neighborhood meeting took place and the main communication line—The Telephone Chain—began in 1975.

Citizens Crime Watch (CCW) received cooperation from local police departments. They instructed citizens on crime prevention and provided information about crimes that occurred in their communities. The people contributed to the reduction of crime and the arrest of suspects by reporting suspicious persons or activities. This joint effort brought citizens and police closer; it opened lines of communication. CCW owes its success as an organization to the team effort of volunteers and police.

COMMUNITY AFFAIRS BUREAU (CAB)

CAB administers a variety of programs designed to foster cooperation between the department and the community. Some of those programs include The Youth Service Section which continues to operate the Drug Abuse Resistance Education (DARE), Police Athletic Leisure (PAL), and "Join A Team Not a Gang" programs to more than 200,000 Miami-Dade County school children. Students are taught the dangers of substance abuse, peer pressure, and gang membership. Officers introduce self-esteem building principles, constructive sports, and recreational activities as viable alternatives to truancy, drug abuse, and gang involvement.

The Community Service Section is responsible for community relations and crime prevention efforts on a countywide basis. The Section is involved in a myriad of departmental, state, and federal programs including the Don't Let Alcohol Be Your Last Taste of Life, Gang Resistance Education and Training (GREAT), Business Against Narcotics and Drugs (BAND), DUI Mobile Education Center, Turn Around Police Academy (TAP), the Educational Police Robot, and the Citizens' Police Academy. There are more than 60 additional initiatives geared toward education, safety, and well-being of residents in the county.

CRIMES RATES

It was reported that violent crime in Miami-Dade County was down by 34% over the five year period ending in 2000. The reports showed 18,549 in 1996 to 12,301 in 2000. Nonviolent crime was also down from 106,038 in 1996 to 72,054 in 2000 or 32%. A few areas of particular interest are that there were 142 homicides in 1996 but 99 in 2000 with a clearance rate of 68%. Robberies went from 6,308 to 3,419 in 2000 and it was reported that that rate is the lowest robbery rate since 1979. DUI fatalities went from a high of 39 in 1998 to 20 in 2000, while young gun deaths went from 48 in 1996 to 16 in 2000. Two other areas seem interesting: Street Terror Offenders Program reports that seizures were shown as:

- 1996: 27 firearms, 82 Kg Narcotics
- 1997: 88 firearms, 348 Kg Narcotics
- 1998: 76 firearms, 48 Kg Narcotics
- 1999: 71 firearms, 28 Kg Narcotics
- 2000: 96 firearms, 73 Kg Narcotics

Finally, Cargo Theft Hijacking Task Force reported recovered property value in 1996 as estimated at $9.9 million as compared to 1999 at $24 million.

MDPD DEPARTMENTAL GOALS, FISCAL YEARS 2000/2001

Goal 1: To provide Miami-Dade County citizens and visitors with comprehensive police services including traditional municipal, specialized investigative, and sheriff's services which ensure public safety. Department will keep pace with population growth and address crime trends to maintain community support and citizen satisfaction.

Goal 2: To continue the reduction of serious and violent crime by implementing aggressive and innovative crime prevention and crime fighting initiatives, and by working cooperatively with other law enforcement agents in this effort.

Goal 3: To implement state-of-the-art, Year 2000 compliant, information technology which directly supports uniform and investigative operations, and to establish management reporting systems that maximize the effective and efficient utilization of resources.

Goal 4: To maintain the highest standards of professional police conduct by emphasizing ethics and integrity in continued compliance with accreditation standards.

MDPD OBJECTIVES, FISCAL YEARS 2000/2001

OBJECTIVE 1: Maintain average emergency response time of less than four minutes. Reduce the number and length of time that non-emergency calls for service are held.

OBJECTIVE 2: Continue to implement proactive, aggressive, crime-fighting initiatives in order to continue the reduction Part I Crimes such as robbery, aggravated assault, burglary, and motor vehicle theft utilizing the Street Terror Offender Program (STOP), Robbery Intervention Detail-Enhanced (RIDE), Tactical Narcotics Team (TNT), Multi-Agency Gang Task Force, (MAGTF), Multi-Agency Auto Theft Task Force (MAATTH), Tactical Operations Multi-Agency Cargo Anti-Theft Squad (TOMCATS) as well as conduct truancy, car criminal enforcement, and warrants sweeps, tourist robbery abatement, and DUI checkpoints activities.

OBJECTIVE 3: Continue to implement Police Services' enhanced enforcement initiatives and innovative crime fight programs to address criminal activities in district neighborhoods including burglary, traffic, automobile theft, prostitution, gangs, narcotics, truancy, and stolen property. COMPSTAT, an in-depth statistical review process of criminal data which identifies emerging crime trends, is utilized in conjunction with the enhanced enforcement programs to provide proactive remediation in specific Miami-Dade County neighborhoods.

OBJECTIVE 4: Continue to investigate allegations of public corruption and misconduct through appropriate dedicated resources and the establishment of cooperative investigative relationships with the Miami-Dade County Inspector General, the Federal Bureau of Investigation, and the Florida Department of Law Enforcement, in addition to other involved law enforcement agencies, with the complete support of both the Dade State Attorney and US Attorney's Offices.

OBJECTIVE 5: Continue community policing programs throughout unincorporated Miami-Dade County to specifically address identified neighborhood needs, and remain responsive to community concerns through positive police-citizen interaction involving Citizen Advisory Committees (CAC), crime and neighborhood war groups, homeowners associations, and other community and civic organizations.

In sum, the MDPD appears to be well organized, controlling crime (see Figure 7.1), reducing the fear of crime, and has in place goals and objectives that seem to lend themselves well to enhancing the quality of life experiences of their community members. However, what do a few of their constituents think?[3]

TESTING POLICE PERFORMANCE
IN MIAMI-DADE COUNTY, FLORIDA

In all, there were 212 surveys completed by residents of Miami-Dade County, Florida who lived in the county for an average of 14 years (see Table 7.1). Their average age was 45. Of the participants, 30 (14%) largely characterized their employment as a blue-collar job, and 80 (38%) as a white-collar job. Thirty-five (17%) said they were retired, 20 (9%) were students, 8 (4%) worked in retail, and 20 (9%) business owners. There were 53 (25%) female and 159 (75%) male respondents. Ninety (43%) described themselves as white, 31 (15%) as black, 66 (31%) as Latino, 4 (2%) as Asian, and 21 (10%) ignored the question.

When they were asked about what homeland they identified with, 137 (65%) reported the USA, 48 (23%) reported Western Europe, and 13 (6%) said it was Haiti, Dominican Republic, or Caribbean. Six (3%) said it was Central or South America or Mexico, and 2 (1%) identified their homeland as Cape Verde or Cuba. Fifty-nine (28%) said they spoke English at home, 35 (17%) spoke English and another language, and 109 (51%) spoke only Spanish or Portuguese. Finally, 62 (29%) said they rented and 133 (63%) owned their home.

TABLE 7.1   Characteristics of Miami-Dade County, Florida Sample, N = 212

	NUMBERS	PERCENTS[*]/RANGE
Length of Time	14 years	1–40 years
Age	45	20–72
Occupation		
Blue Collar	30	14%
White Collar	80	38%
Retired	35	17%
Student	20	9%
Retail	8	4%
Business Owner	20	9%
Other/Missing	19	9%
Gender		
Females	53	25%
Males	159	75%
Race		
White	90	43%
Black	31	15%
Latino	66	31%
Asian	4	2%
Missing	21	10%
Homeland		
Western Europe	48	23%
Eastern Europe	0	0%
Haiti/Dominican/Caribbean	13	6%
Central/South America/Mexico	6	3%
Cape Verde/Cuba	2	1%
China/Asia	0	0%
USA	137	65%
Language Spoken Home		
English	59	28%
English and another language	35	17%
Only Spanish or Portuguese	109	51%
Other/Missing	9	4%
Residents		
Rented	62	29%
Owned	133	63%
Lived with others	0	0%

[*]All percents rounded. Missing cases not always included.

MAKING DECISIONS AND MEETINGS

The sample overwhelmingly reported that they were not involved in any decision-making processes conducted by MDPD. However, 156 (74%) reported they would participate in police discussions, if asked.

At community meetings, 103 (49%) said that often or sometimes community members worked together. Although, 91 (43%) said that seldom or never were neighborhood people encouraged to attend community policing meetings. Also, 95 (45%) reported that seldom or never did they leave a meeting with a to-do list, and 134 (63%) reported they seldom or never helped to develop problem-solving remedies. At many meetings, while respondents revealed police had not monopolized those meetings with one-way conversations about enforcement, but very often previous problem solving plans changed to fit new findings. Only, 36 (17%) respondents reported they were sure solutions coming from problem solving discussions were practical. But, 152 (72%) reported solutions were impractical or they weren't sure.

CHANGES

When Miami-Dade survey takers were asked in what way their community was safer since the community started meetings (as opposed to the participant attending meetings), many comments were offered but the most important comment shared by 40% (85) of the sample was that response time of officers was about the same. Also, 91 (43%) survey takers said they didn't know how police contributed to their safety. However, 56 (26%) suggested it had not been long enough to tell.

GREATEST NEIGHBORHOOD PROBLEMS

The 212 Miami-Dade residents reported their most serious community issues were:

- Home invasion
- Streets, lights, empty buildings, and graffiti
- Gangs and juveniles
- Street drug activity
- Fear or lack of trust of police
- Parking, traffic, and speeders
- Panhandlers and prostitutes
- No problem or others

Specifically, 68 (32%) said their most serious neighborhood problem was home invasion, and 37 (18%) reported it as streets, lights, empty buildings, and graffiti.

Thirty-five (17%) said it was gangs and juveniles, and 28 (13%) said it was street drug activity. Eighteen (9%) reported it as fear or lack of trust of police, 13 (6%) reported it as parking, traffic, and speeders, and finally, 9 (4%) said it was panhandlers and prostitutes.

REMEDIES

When 212 Miami-Dade participants were asked how to curb those problems, the following responses were offered:

- Quality policing and municipal services
- Homeownership and business investment

Ninety-six (45%) residents reported the best way to solve community problems was to deliver quality police and municipal services. Quality referred to more than service, it referred to the personnel delivering services and often, it was clear that "who" took precedence over "what." From the evidence, it appeared the relationship between officers and community, while not a conflictual or aggressive relationship, was one of co-existence. While officers seemed to share an "ear but not a heart" with the community, one participant wrote, "we are here to stay." Participants argued that officers and municipal workers from a different culture than their own hardly understood the community's needs, issues, or relationships. Their thinking went along the lines of, "How do outsiders solve inside crime," one participant clarified. They felt so strongly about this idea that many participants wrote that officers and municipal workers should live in the communities where they work.

These participants did not reject other cultures, but their point was that few arrests were made concerning home invasions and crimes of violence in their communities. Investigators who really didn't understand the community, they argued, had trouble in putting together a case to make an arrest. Because of this shared idea, many participants never reported crimes, and others were arrested, some said, for crimes they didn't commit. For instance, a few participants didn't deny they committed a crime or two, but some of them were wrongfully accused of crimes (home invasion and aggravated assault). Ten percent of the participants were arrested at one time or another, and two were convicted and one still awaited trial. There was some speculation that police services and municipal services were withheld because their communities were not as affluent or as "white as other neighborhoods." Class issues were offered by the participants to explain why police services—especially criminal investigators—were outsiders.

A similar idea was shared about municipal personnel, too. Services were delivered that were unnecessary, and necessary services were unavailable, they argued. A belief held by many respondents was that county decision makers knew little about the real needs of the communities within the county. For example, although the school system in Miami-Dade was highly regarded and promoted the values of the community, the school curriculum rarely reflected their cultural values from their perspective. That is, the cultural viewpoints celebrated by the public school system as an achievement in cultural strides were from an American vision of their cultural perspectives.

Also, 47 (22%) said that home ownership and business investment was one way to solve some of their serious community issues. That is, generally, residents who lived in neighborhoods were all culturally similar, and rarely were people of different cultures living together. That there would be a block of Dominicans joined to a block of Puerto Ricans and another block might consist of people from Central America was the implication. Their main issue concerning housing was that their property values would remain lower if all Haitians, for example, lived in a community. They wanted the community opened to others for two reasons: 1) to enhance their property equity, and 2) to increase their "say-so" and resources of their schools which seemed to be great priorities. They felt the schools were not furthering their cultural heritage, which they were exceptionally proud of, but American mainstream ideas. They felt part of their heritage, and for some, the biggest part of their heritage was their American connection.

In business, some of their concerns were that large businesses should move into the community and dispose of the small businesses that shared a different set of cultural ideas about service, products, and relationships than the community they served. They wrote about bridging cultural barriers. It was their perspective that business had to change, not them. After all, "I'm the customer," a respondent wrote.

The community members polled revealed other conceptual thoughts that can be divided into three central themes that seem to be linked together:

- Police and municipal oversight committees
- Police and other city departments work together
- Political power

One hundred and five residents (50%) furthered their thoughts about ways to solve community problems which characterized oversight committee participation. That is, while over a third of them reported the police put them at ease when they came into contact with officers, one-half of the survey takers thought that by guiding police conduct through oversight committees, neighborhood problems would be addressed in an advantageous manner. The survey takers were saying that bridging the cultural gap between cultures could be accomplished if the community had more control over police hiring, training, practice, priorities, discipline, and promotions. The point is that community members no longer wanted to try to understand the personnel employed by the county, they wanted those employees to work, in part, under their direction.

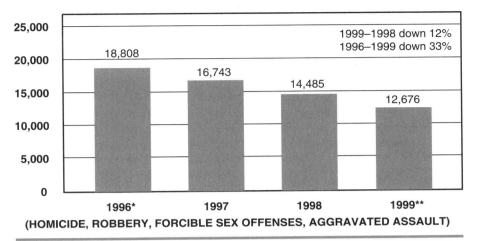

FIGURE 7.1   Miami-Dade Police Department Violent Crimes
*Operation Safe Streets/Clean Sweep Implemented December 1996.
**January–December 29, 1999.
Source: MDPD Uniform Crime Reports, MDPD Crime Analysis System.

Also, 57 (27%) said that the police and other county departments should work together to provide services for their community. In this case, participants emphasized county services such as trash pickups, speed bumps, health centers, and city cleanup of parks, streets, and schools. One repetitious issue among their answers was the concern that throughout the county, others received better county services including police service, and they wanted similar services. This thought is consistent with one method they said would aid them in county services, which was political involvement. Specifically, 46 (22%) said they wanted more control over the political process of the county that included issues concerning decisions that impacted their community. The participants had little interest in actively participating in countywide decisions.

SAFETY

Twenty-four (11%) said that they felt unsafe today as compared to a year ago, and 89 (42%) said nothing had changed. But, 27 (13%) reported it was safer in their neighborhood as compared to last year; in fact, 72 (34%) said it was much safer.

POLICE PERFORMANCE RATED

Based on the experience the residents had with police officer(s):

- 73 (34%) rated police performance as professional
- 67 (32%) rated police performance as fair
- 51 (25%) rated police performance as frightening or intimidating

Also, when they commented on the performance of officers at a crime or accident scene, 80 (38%) said response time was good or excellent, 68 (32%) said officers solved the problem, 72 (34%) said officers put them at ease, 77 (36%) said officers were helpful, but only 46 (21%) said officers were dressed appropriately.

POLICE EFFECTIVENESS

When participants were asked how effective the MDPD was in responding to neighborhood problems, findings revealed the MDPD was:

- Effective or very effective: 35 (17%)
- Ineffective: 135 (64%)
- Didn't know: 19 (9%)
- Police had their own agenda: 23 (11%)

What else did the respondents think? They thought specific officers should spend more time making personal contact with community residents, more officers should be assigned to a neighborhood on a long-term basis, and that many more should work in the schools of the community. But, almost one-half of them said the police talked down to them although many thought the police listened to their non-criminal concerns. Also, 127 (60%) residents reported that they were comfortable in taking their suggestions or complaints to the police, and most felt making the community safe should be a joint effort between police and residents.

THE FUTURE

When the participants were asked about the future, they reported that all things being equal, the neighborhood a year from now would be:

- A better place to live: 17 (8%)
- Will stay about the same: 70 (33%)
- A worse place to live: 81 (38%)
- Not sure about its future: 44 (21%)

SUMMARY

A historical account and the demographic characteristics of Miami-Dade County and its police department were described, and its director's statement about the police agency and their community police strategies were offered. The events that helped shape the Citizens Crime Watch were highlighted, followed by an examination of the Community Affairs Bureau, crime rates, and departmental goals and objectives for fiscal years 2000–2001. Finally, results from a survey consisting of 212 participants were presented to determine if the Miami-Dade Police Department was meeting community police objectives.

The participants consisted primarily of middle-aged males, many of whom held white-collar jobs and described themselves as either white or Latino. Most owned their own home and over one-half of them only spoke Spanish while at home. Although many of the respondents would participate in a police decision-making process, few had an opportunity to do so. Their greatest concerns were home invasion, streets, lights, empty buildings, graffiti, and gangs including juveniles. Quality policing and city services were their most serious remedies to curb community problems, but they were more concerned with "who" delivered police services as opposed to "what" services were delivered. Concerning municipal services, the issues were both what and who. They argued that the police cleared few home invasions and other crimes because the police investigators did not understand their culture; consequently, few crimes were reported and many said that wrongful arrest was pervasive in their community. They did reveal that social class was an issue concerning appropriate police and county services. Many rated police officers as professional but rated the agency as ineffective in dealing with neighborhood issues. Very few felt their future would be better, and most felt that things would probably stay the same.

CONCLUSION: MIAMI-DADE COUNTY

Based on the evidence produced by 212 residents of Miami-Dade County and the public records of both Miami-Dade County and the Miami-Dade Police Department, it appears that reported crime especially homicide and robberies along with DUI fatalities were down. However, the community members polled lived in fear of crime, and consequently their quality of life experiences seemed suspect.

To answer the primary question under investigation: does police practice enhance neighborhood safety issues and provide social order or stability? Before the investigation, it was believed that community police strategies give rise to crime control, reductions in the fear of crime, and enhancements in resident quality of life experiences. After reviewing the findings from the investigation, that belief was rejected.

First of all there was little evidence that any of the constituents influenced police decision-making processes. There was little support that community members regardless of their cultural diversity influenced the police at any level, therefore public order was not necessarily enhanced due to a community policing effort in the county.

Neighborhood issues and police issues might at first glance appear to be similar yet a closer look suggests that there are two separate issues to consider. While the MDPD focused on crime control and police efficiency, participants rated the MDPD as inefficient problem-solvers. Community members were fearful of living in their neighborhoods, doubtful about their future safety, rejected official police intrusion into the lives of their children, and reported crime less often than expected. The fear of crime, home invasion issues, ideas that police investigators had not cleared many of those home invasions with an arrest, produced fewer reports and certainly would have impacted their confidence in the police. When an arrest was made, it was a local community member arrested, and what was argued, in part, was investigators arrested whomever was convenient. That is, they argued, police investigators who lacked the knowledge of the community's cultural nuances would be less capable of solving crime and coming up with the real culprits. Community members implied that while the MDPD showed lower crime rates and more arrests, those lower crime rates were due in part to fewer reports made by the community, and more arrests were a result of an exploitable population. There was little evidence to suggest the exploitation was intentional, but rather a product of cultural ignorance on the part of the investigators. Wrongful arrests were evidently pervasive through the communities surveyed—or at least, this is one way to explain the thoughts of the residents. One problem is it is hard to tell what's real and what's not. If they think something is real, it is. That is, they live in fear of home invasion and in fear of a wrongful arrest.

To solve their most serious neighborhood problem and this dilemma, participants argued that the department needs to widen their cultural understanding and maintain local residents as officers and investigators and empower community members on oversight committees.

A similar perspective seemed to be present among the participants concerning all county personnel, especially education personnel. Public school curriculum, for instance, was powered by an American version of knowledge and consequently, they as well as the youth in their community were resentful of the American version. Municipal services did not focus on their needs or their concerns. Yet, participants made it clear that while they appreciated and respected American ideals, they would not disavow their cultural heritage as evidenced, in part, through the high percentage of respondents who only speak Spanish at home. They would not encourage an Americanization of their youth primarily because American youths, they said, had greater access to drugs, were disrespectful towards elders and religion, and were more independent of family obligations and responsibilities. For those reasons, they wanted selective enforcement of youths—enforce the laws towards outsiders. Miami-Dade County was home, but their culture and heritage were their souls.

ENDNOTES

1. See US Census Website at: http//www. census.gov.

2. See Miami-Dade Police Department's Website for more detail: http://www.mdpd.com/.

3. The survey findings which followed were distributed and collected by Lt. Gerald A. Rudoff MDPD, Community Affairs Buearu and Professor Ellen G. Cohn at the Florida International University. However, many surveys were distributed by community college students in the county.

TESTING POLICE PERFORMANCE IN MIDLAND, TEXAS

INTRODUCTION

Midland, Texas was selected as part of this investigation because of its "official" concern for cultural diversity as reported by the city's Website.[1] Yet, as the home of President George W. Bush, Midland might have some interesting issues to consider.

Midland, Texas is located in west Texas, the Land of the High Sky, where clean air and sunshine are abundant.[2] In 2000, Midland was home to approximately 95,000 people living in 65 square miles of which approximately 72,000 (76%) were white, 27,543 (29%) represented a Hispanic or Latino population (some are white), and 7,800 (8%) represented a black or African American population.[3] The city is midway between Fort Worth and El Paso along Interstate Highway 20 and is situated approximately 200 miles from the American-Mexican border. Midland serves as an administrative center for the petroleum-producing region known as the Permian Basin, where about 20 percent of America's oil and gas reserves are located. As a management center, the city's demographics reflect a unique concentration of highly-trained and educated people whose incomes, professions, and personal lifestyles demand and receive high levels of service.[4]

MISSION STATEMENT

"We, the members of the Midland Police Department, are committed to being responsive to our community in the delivery of quality service. Recognizing our responsibility to maintain order, while affording dignity and respect to every individual, our objective is to improve the quality of life through a community partnership which promotes safe, secure neighborhoods. The values of the Midland Police Department evolve around People, Leadership, Service and Performance."

HISTORY OF POLICE DEPARTMENT

Until 1941, law enforcement duties in Midland were under the auspices of a town marshal. A growing population required the establishment of the Midland Police Department[5] (MPD) which consisted of seven officers. The communication system consisted of one red light atop the tall Petroleum Building located in downtown Midland. In 1942, the communication system was vastly improved with the installation of modern two-way radio equipment. Both roving cars worked from 7:00 a.m. to 3:00 a.m. By 1947, the department consisted of three patrol cars, twelve officers, and a chief. Midland's city population had reached 23,000 caused by a surging oil boom.

In 1950, the Chief reorganized the 31 man police department into four divisions: Patrol, Special Services, Traffic, and Detectives. By 1953, the MPD totaled forty-five personnel and was equipped with nine patrol cars and five Harley-Davidson motorcycles, each equipped with modern three-way radios. That year, the agency moved into a new Public Safety Building that housed the agency and a 70-prisoner jail. This new jail replaced the two-cell jail that often held up to 45 prisoners.

In 1958, the department had almost doubled in size, and they operated a police academy, brought in police dogs, and purchased 12 police cars. During the mid-1970s, Midland police officers shot and killed six suspects in separate incidents. An officer was shot and seriously injured by a burglary suspect. The MPD was challenged to combat this growing crime rate.

During the early 1980s, Midland experienced an economic "boom." An increased population brought a higher number of calls for service. When the "boom" ended in 1985, the agency suffered its own "bust," with officers resigning or retiring in record numbers, and they were not replaced due to financial cutbacks. Police divisions were reorganized, and Midland voters approved a public safety bond proposal which provided for a new Communications Center equipped with state of the art equipment. The center included a CAD (Computer Aided Dispatch) System. In 1993, the Midland Police Department became the 270th law enforcement agency to be nationally accredited.

In 1995, an investigation showed that a gang problem existed in Midland, and was increasing in severity and membership. Products of these gangs included drive-by shootings, along with fights, criminal mischief, and assaults. It became apparent that a more proactive enforcement was necessary. As a result, the MPD Gang Suppression Unit was developed.

The MPD implemented their Problem Oriented Policing philosophy in 1996 with the purchase of a 35-foot vehicle to be used as a mobile substation. Three officers and a supervisor were assigned to the substation and were funded by the President's Cops Ahead Grant. The substation was set up in a "strategic location" within a challenged neighborhood and served toward making "the neighborhood more self-reliant." The MPD is organized by function into four bureaus: Field

tions, Investigative Services, Support Services, and Administrative Services. There were 159 sworn officers and 51 civilians employed by the MPD in early 2001. That is approximately one sworn officer for every 600 residents.

CRIME IN MIDLAND

Table 8.1 shows the number and types of Part I Crime for 1993–1998 for Midland, Texas. Crime information reports supplied by the MPD showed only crimes that were categorized as Part I Crimes by the FBI's Uniform Crime Report. The differences between 1993 and 1998 reflected 973 crimes or 194% for six years or what can be 32% per year decrease in the crimes reported.

To better understand the significance of those crimes rates, in the State of Texas during the calendar year of 1997 there were an estimated 1,064,914 Part I Crimes reported. In 1997 violent crimes made up 11 percent of the total index of crimes of the state. The remaining 89% was composed of property crimes. The 1997 total crime volume in Texas decreased 2.5% as compared to 1996.

Table 8.2 compares the number and types of 1998 Part I Crimes that occurred in Midland, Texas with cities geographically close. It appears that based on the reported crimes of those five cities, Midland had the lowest crime rate in 1997. Also, a close examination reveals that Midland has a crime rate of 40.02 in 1998 as compared to 46.68 in 1997 based on Part I Crimes. Violent crime rates—at least based on the crimes emphasized—Midland had the lowest crime rate among them.

FAMILY VIOLENCE

The Texas Family Code defines family violence as an act by a member of a family or household against another member that is intended to result in physical harm,

TABLE 8.1　Part I Crimes

PART I CRIMES	1993	1994	1995	1996	1997	1998
Murder	8	9	9	4	5	2
Sexual Assault	76	67	68	57	80	79
Robbery	79	89	88	79	89	66
Aggravated Assault	243	368	312	232	234	209
Burglary	1,062	1,083	1,004	1,030	950	798
Theft	3,227	3,256	3,074	3,273	3,171	2,640
Auto Theft	328	207	290	286	219	256
Totals	5,023	5,079	4,845	4,961	4,748	4,050

TABLE 8.2   Five City Crime Comparison Rate: 1997

TYPE OF CRIME	ABILENE	LUBBOCK	MIDLAND	ODESSA	SAN ANGELO
Murder	2	6	5	5	0
Sexual Assault	67	92	80	27	54
Robbery	124	220	89	121	33
Aggravated Assault	449	1,518	234	666	316
Burglary	1,320	2,588	950	1,063	666
Theft	4,147	7,644	3,171	3,545	3,715
Auto Theft	294	699	219	299	160
Totals	6,430	12,767	4,748	5,656	4,944
Estimated Population	116,384	205,694	101,714	100,233	93,847
Crime Rate	55.02	62.07	46.68	56.43	52.68

bodily injury, or assault, or a threat that reasonably places the member in fear of imminent physical harm. By definition and for the purposes of family violence reports, "family" includes individuals related by consanguinity (blood) or affinity, marriage or former marriage, biological parents of the same child, and members or former members of the same household (including roommates).

The largest percentage of family violence reports was between married spouses. The second most commonly reported relationship among offenders and victims was common-law spouses, and the third most common relationship was roommates. Although there were 671 reports of family violence investigated by the MPD, when that rate is compared with similar cities, it appears that family violence rates in Midland are not as great a problem in comparison.

Disturbance calls were the next most frequent type of calls for service. Of those calls, 2,171 (39.92%) were basic disturbance calls as compared to 2,578 (47.40%) domestic/family violence calls. In 1997 Midland police officers also responded to 555 (10.20%) disturbance fights and 135 (2.48%) disturbance calls where weapons were used. The average time an officer spent on a disturbance call in 1997 was 21 minutes.

COMMUNITY RELATIONS AND MPD PROGRAMS

The MPD Community Relations Unit is charged with the responsibility of establishing positive communication between the communities and the MPD. While all police officers are obligated to project a positive and professional image of the

TABLE 8.3   Family Violence Incident Reports: 1997

	ABILENE	LUBBOCK	MIDLAND	ODESSA	SAN ANGELO
Number of Incidents	1,533	3,055	671	1,526	1,364
Estimated Population	116,384	205,694	101,714	100,233	93,847
Family Violence Rate	13.17	14.85	6.60	15.22	14.53

department, the MPD Community Relations Unit assists and creates avenues in which to accomplish this task.

Their area of responsibility includes attending seminars, discussions, meetings, demonstrations, and displays. This unit is not isolated in their own area, but is a gathering point for input from all MPD personnel and community members. This input may consist of technical assistance, expert speakers, and suggestions for improving current programs and creating additional ones.

The MPD operates the Citizen Police Academy (CPA). This program is designed to educate citizens on the inner workings of the department. It's a 14-week program with evening classes that is offered twice a year. It is free of charge. Mirroring the CPA is the Spanish Speaking Citizen Police Academy. All instruction is in Spanish.

Other programs include: Neighborhood Watch, Home and Apartment Security Survey, Home Insurance Surveys, Business Survey, Personal Awareness, Fraud and Con Games (targeted to senior citizens), Shoplifting (given to employers), Fingerprinting (of children ages 1–12 for family records), Bicycle Rodeo, McGruff the Crime Dog, Robot Program, Stranger Danger (geared toward children pre-school to 6th grade, helps latch-key children), Hard Hats for Little Heads (police officers, in partnership with the Midland County Medical Society (MCMS), dispense bicycle safety helmets after completion of a bicycle safety program), "WHO DONE IT?" (a crime scene mystery), Kops for Kids Trading Cards, Midland Night Out, and a Halloween Safety Program.

A LOCAL STUDY

A researcher who measured race and ethnicity in Midland found that the majority of police experiences were citizen-initiated as compared to police-initiated contacts.[6] Among the significant findings were:

1. Citizens who initiated police contact viewed police performance more favorably than those whose contacts were initiated by the Odessa and Midland police

2. Police contact was likely to result from a service aspect of policing more than a crime fighting function, and positive police experience not only yielded positive attitudes toward the police, but also neutralized or ameliorated the negative attitudes of citizens

3. Spanish speaking Hispanics felt more satisfied with police performance than whites and English speaking Hispanics

4. Blacks had less favorable attitudes toward police than either whites or the two Hispanic groups

This study concluded that appropriate police policies must be implemented to create positive police–citizen contacts and to enhance police–minority relationships. In another study of the Midland, Texas area, 581 residents were randomly interviewed by telephone.[7] Among significant findings were:

1. Compared to English speaking Hispanics, Spanish speaking Hispanics and whites were more likely to cooperate with the police

2. Spanish speaking Hispanics were more likely to agree with the concept of a house visit by a police officer

3. Spanish speaking Hispanics felt more comfortable talking with an officer who had the same ethnic background, expressed a greater desire to become police officers compared to whites and blacks, and more likely believed that excessive use of force by the police existed in their neighborhoods as compared to whites

In one sense, the findings were not necessarily supported by other research which showed that Hispanics in Texas:[8]

1. Evaluated police less favorably than the general public

2. Were more fearful of crime than the general public

3. Felt that they received inadequate police protection

4. Believed that officers had negative attitudes and discriminated against Hispanics

What were the findings from an investigation recently conducted for *Applied Community Policing in the 21st Century*?

TESTING POLICE PERFORMANCE IN MIDLAND, TEXAS

There were 213 surveys completed by residents of Midland. They reported that they lived in Midland for an average of 11 years (see Table 8.4). Their average age was 42.

Thirty-three (16%) described their employment as blue-collar work and 40 (19%) described it as white-collar work. Thirty-one (15%) were retired, 18 (8%) were students, 11 (5%) worked in retail establishments, and 36 (17%) were business owners. There were 44 (21%) missing cases.

There were 122 (57%) female and 87 (41%) male respondents. Fourteen (7%) described themselves as white, 33 (16%) as black, 121 (57%) as Latino, 6 (3%) as Asian, and 39 (18%) didn't answer the question.

When participants were asked which country best represented their homeland, most (127, 60%) said Central or South America and/or Mexico. Also, 51 (24%) reported it was Western Europe, 27 (13%) reported Haiti, the Dominican Republic, or the Caribbean. Few reported the USA or China/Asia as their homeland.

Fifty-nine (28%) said they spoke English at home, 74 (35%) spoke English and another language, and 70 (33%) spoke only Spanish or Portuguese. Finally, 83 (39%) said they rented, 116 (55%) owned their home, and 14 (7%) lived with others.

MAKING DECISIONS AND MEETINGS

Rarely did Midland participants report an involvement in any of the decision-making processes conducted by the police in this investigation.[9] And, 85 (40%) participants reported they did not know if they were willing to participate in any discussions, yet almost one-half of the remaining respondents reported they were willing to participate.

At community meetings, over one-half of them reported community members seldom or never worked together. Also, 87 (41%) reported that seldom or never were neighborhood people encouraged to attend community policing meetings. Also, 120 (56%) reported that seldom or never had they left a meeting with a to-do list, and 73 (34%) reported they had seldom or never helped develop their own problem solving remedies. Respondents revealed Midland police monopolized meetings with enforcement concerns, and seldom or never were previous problem solving plans changed to fit new findings. Only, 22 (10%) reported they were sure solutions coming from problem solving discussions were practical. On the other hand, 151 (71%) reported solutions were impractical solutions or they weren't sure.

CHANGES

When Midland survey takers were asked in what way their community was safer since the community started meeting (as opposed to the participant attending meetings), many comments were offered which fit the following categories:

TABLE 8.4   Characteristics of Midland, Texas Sample, N = 213

	NUMBERS	PERCENTS[*]/RANGE
Length of Time	11 years	0–40 years
Age	42	19–66
Occupation		
Blue Collar	33	16%
White Collar	40	19%
Retired	31	15%
Student	18	8%
Retail	11	5%
Business Owner	36	17%
Other/Missing	44	21%
Gender		
Females	122	57%
Males	87	41%
Race		
White	14	7%
Black	33	16%
Latino	121	57%
Asian	6	3%
Missing	39	18%
Homeland		
Western Europe	51	24%
Eastern Europe	0	0%
Haiti/Dominican/Caribbean	27	13%
Central/South America/Mexico	127	60%
Cape Verde/Cuba	0	0%
China/Asia	4	2%
USA	4	2%
Language Spoken Home		
English	59	28%
English and another language	74	35%
Only Spanish or Portuguese	70	33%
Other/Missing	10	5%
Residents		
Rented	83	39%
Owned	116	55%
Lived with others	14	7%

[*]All percents rounded. Missing cases not always included.

- Response time of officers was about the same: 50 (24%)
- People who previously remained quiet about crime now talked about it: 81 (38%)
- People now helped the police do their job: 47 (22%)
- Officers now felt part of the neighborhood: 6 (3%)
- Didn't know or offered no comment: 29 (14%)

Finally, 92 (43%) survey takers reported they didn't know how Midland police contributed to their safety.

GREATEST NEIGHBORHOOD PROBLEMS

The 213 Midland participants reported their most serious neighborhood issue was:

- Fear or lack of trust of police
- Home invasion
- Streets, lights, empty buildings, and graffiti
- No problem or other
- Panhandlers and prostitutes
- Street drug activity
- Gangs and juveniles
- Parking, traffic, and speeders

Specifically, 75 (35%) participants reported their greatest neighborhood problem related to fear or lack of trust of police, and 37 (17%) said home invasion, followed by 34 (16%) who reported streets, lights, empty buildings, and graffiti. Thirty-one (15%) reported that there was no large neighborhood problem, and 14 (7%) reported panhandlers and prostitutes were the greatest problems of the community. There was a numeric tie between gangs and street drug activity—each with 9 (5%) survey takers reporting those events. Finally, 4 (2%) respondents reported it was parking, traffic, and speeding. Other problems included retail stores selling products at excessively high prices, juvenile bike riders and skate boards, and public parks crowded with youths who engaged in fights and drugs. Poor burial services, absence of public transportation, schools and health services dominated by "Anglo" ideals, and city and social agencies that interacted with many of the participants and/or their friends and family members as though they were "stupid" were also cited as problems.

REMEDIES

When the Midland participants were asked what should be done to curb those neighborhood problems, the following responses were offered:

■ Homeownership and business investment
■ Quality policing and municipal services

Remedies for Midland's most serious neighborhood problems centered on issues not of law enforcement but of their homes and business establishments who catered to them. That is, the best way to curb neighborhood problems, 88 (41%) residents reported, was through home ownership issues and business reinvestment into the neighborhood. For instance, homes they owned were in need of repair, and although they took pride in them and wanted privacy, they felt vulnerable to outside focus. When homes required repairs, city inspectors could intrude on their privacy, they argued. Also, many felt the value of their property did not increase at a similar rate as other homes in Midland. Therefore, they felt their net worth was not increasing as rapidly as other homeowners' and should they wish to purchase a new home, the equity wasn't there as expected. Some participants added that their housing market was different than housing markets throughout the city. They received fewer rewards, had more difficulty when transferring deeds, and were in a buyers' market rather than a sellers' market.

Then, too, borrowing money on their homes to enhance their properties was a task in comparison to other residents of Midland. Because their homes needed repair, city inspectors and "unknown" city workers confronted them "at their front door" and many felt that they did not enjoy the same privacy and control over their property as other residents. One recurring thought reported by the participants was they sacrificed much throughout their lives to afford their home. Furthermore, home ownership was an ultimate level of achievement—it was as though, "owning a home is the most important accomplishment in my life," wrote one resident. Yet, at any time, they could come under attack by authorities and lose it. This thought is consistent with their fear or lack of trust of the police.

Homeownership was more than a personal accomplishment. Homeownership translated to family success in that the life chances of their children were improved and both their own personal and family status within their community was enhanced. For those reasons, among other reasons, participants who rented wanted options to purchase a home, too. Those options should not be construed to mean welfare since "handouts, for (competent) hard working people," was seen as a "deception" and therefore welfare or what they called handouts could produce disrespect from family members and the community at large. In part, this was consistent with Miami-Dade County residents despite the fact that most of those residents saw the USA as their homeland as compared to Midland respondents who saw Central/South America or Mexico as theirs. Yet in both samples, Spanish was the predominant language spoken at home.[10]

Also, 58 (27%) survey takers reported "other" as their answer in solving neighborhood problems. There were 25 different answers that did not fit into a single theme category. Some of those ideas included more health care, frequent trash pickups, maintenance of parks and schools, centers for youth (under community direction), criminal screening of door-to-door peddlers and local businesses, more family oriented events, and greater links with neighborhood schools. There were eight school related thoughts in their responses that focused on everything from quality teachers, transportation for their children, quality food services, supervised (not a law enforcement presence) sporting events, and courses that related more to their cultural perspectives than "Anglo" perspectives.

Quality police and city services were reported by 47 (22%) participants as their solution to serious neighborhood problems. They wrote about enforcement and punitive action toward violent violators who committed crimes of homicide, aggravated assault, sexual assault, and armed robbery. Drug traffickers, alcoholism, and drug addiction were not seen as crimes of violence by this population. The participants wanted increased neighborhood patrols that pursued low-tolerance intrusion but toward outside violators and youths who lived in other communities. They wanted police to guide their youth (inform them of the law) as opposed to "enforce laws." This finding suggests that their youth were either not a problem or the participants preferred police preventive interaction with their children. This thought, too, might be centered in their fear or lack of trust of the police.

The community members revealed thoughts that could be divided into two central themes:

- Political involvement
- Police and other city departments working together

One hundred (47%) Midland residents furthered their thoughts about solving their neighborhood problems through political involvement with city government. That is, they had little reason to trust their political city leaders and wanted better representation in the political arena. However, of greater importance, they wanted access to city departments to enhance their neighborhoods which meant to enhance their homes in order to provide greater life chances for their children and add a little something to their personal status. They tolerated current city services because they felt disconnected and isolated. A typical thought clarified this point: "Everything with the city is a fight." They wanted the city and police to work together as a single unit, reported 47 (22%) survey takers, and felt that police and city agencies were often "the very depths of our situation."

SAFETY

When they were asked how safe it was to live in their neighborhood as compared to a year before this survey was taken, 124 (58%) reported they felt unsafe. Nothing changed, reported 49 (23%) survey takers. Yet, 20 (9%) reported they felt safer than they had a year ago.

POLICE PERFORMANCE RATED

Based on the experience a participant had with police:

- 82 (39%) rated police performance as professional
- 73 (34%) rated police performance as fair
- 36 (18%) rated police performance as frightening or intimidating
- 22 (10%) missing

When officers responded to calls of service at a crime or accident scene, 120 (56%) participants said response time was good or excellent, 102 (48%) said the officer(s) solved the problem, 125 (59%) said the officer(s) put them at ease, 110 (52%) said the officer(s) were helpful, and 114 (54%) said the officer(s) were dressed appropriately. In each case, approximately 12% ignored the question. Police officer performance was rated high.

POLICE EFFECTIVENESS

When participants were asked how effective the department was in responding to neighborhood problems, the findings revealed the department was:

- Effective or very effective: 117 (55%)
- Ineffective: 83 (39%)
- Didn't know: 60 (28%)
- Police have their own agenda: 17 (8%)

What else did the respondents think? Nine of every ten of them thought police should spend more time making personal contact with neighborhood residents. Eight of every ten strongly agreed that police should be assigned to a neighborhood on a long-term basis, and seven of every ten thought police should be more involved with school activities. Also, 80 (37%) thought police talked down to them, but many thought the police listened to their non-criminal concerns. But, 93 (45%) survey takers reported they were uncomfortable in taking their suggestions or complaints to the police, yet, another 91 (43%) said they felt okay in taking their complaints to the police.

THE FUTURE

When the participants were asked about the future, they reported the neighborhood a year from now would be:

- A better place to live: 6 (3%)
- Will stay about the same: 69 (32%)
- A worse place to live: 88 (41%)
- Not sure about its future: 50 (24%)

SUMMARY

Demographics of Midland, Texas were reviewed. It was noted that many of the respondents spoke English and another language or only another language in their homes most often, Central or South America or Mexico was reported as their homeland most often, and they described their race as Latino most often. Also, there were many more women than men polled, and most of them owned their homes as opposed to renting them. Their largest neighborhood problems were fear or mistrust of the police followed by home invasion. Action recommended included home ownership issues in the sense of their property's equity and intervention from city agencies. Although they gave individual Midland police officers high grades for performance and the department high grades for community involvement, they reported their future looked doubtful.

CONCLUSION: MIDLAND, TEXAS

Based on the evidence provided by 213 Midland residents and the public records of both the city of Midland and the Midland Police Department, reported crimes of violence for the years evaluated were reduced, but the fear of crime was ever present among Midland survey takers. They saw little chance of change. Quality of life issues seemed suspect due in part to an uncertainty about their future and lack of influence and confidence over city services including their own personal safety and the outcomes of their children. While they were proud of their neighborhoods and homes, there was a general feeling of isolation from city services and many residents felt deprived of services they thought were delivered throughout the city except where they lived. The first impression that comes to mind is that they were subject to constant official intrusion due to their location within in the social structure of Midland. Homes in general allowed for greater privacy, but their homes required repair and consequently, city inspectors often intruded in their lives. Many residents felt uncomfortable with city personnel and policy and were uncertain about police officers even to the point of suggesting that their most serious problem was the police.

Also, they sought police guidance of their young and wanted police to aid their children in understanding the law, yet they rejected police enforcement of their children implying a lack of confidence in the justice system. Perhaps some of their lack of confidence was centered around police decisions to target specific neighborhoods with greater surveillance using community police perspectives as a ploy. In part, this idea could have been developed when the department moved a 35-foot police trailer into challenged neighborhoods and called those mini-stations community police centers.

Therefore, to answer the primary question under investigation: does police practice enhance neighborhood safety issues and provide social order or stability? In this case it appears that police intrusion in the communities surveyed produced social disorder. Furthermore, it was believed prior to the investigation community that police strategies gave rise to crime control, reduced the fear of crime, and enhanced resident quality of life experiences. However, this thought apparently was not supported by the data. It was also assumed that if community members, especially culturally diverse members, influenced the decisions of the police, the likelihood that public safety and lifestyle experiences would be enhanced was greater. And again, this idea was not supported by the data. In fact, there was little evidence suggesting that culturally diverse community members engaged in any police decision-making processes in Midland.

It would appear that most of the survey takers had issues with both the Midland city public service and police practice. Some of those issues seemed centered around a mistrust the participants held about public policy, and not the actual personnel who represented the city including police officers whom they felt to be highly professional in their duties. There also appears to be a frustration among the sample as they described what appeared to be a Catch-22 effect; that is, their properties were in need of repair, and they were denied a home equity loan to aid them in that repair because their property was in need of repair. In part, they saw this dilemma as a failure on the part of the city to provide assistance. Evidently, they might not have been as sophisticated as a group about finances. This insecurity in city government evidently promoted "lip service" to city matters as opposed to their serious involvement with government. What appears to be happening is that the sample remained aloof from city government and city government obliged their implied request doing little to help link them with city resources. Thus, it would be easy to understand why one of the respondents implied that there was a great deal of segregation between Hispanics (Latinos) and others. In order for Midland to serve and protect through a community police model, there are walls that must come down, and it is a great opportunity for police policy to assume a leadership role since they are the guardians of the city. But in a final analysis there is more to this story. That is, why would residents be fearful or lack confidence in the police when they have high regards for officers individually? In part this answer was addressed in Chapter 1 of this work.

What was suggested amounted to an idea that Midland suffered from a similar experience to that of Camden, NJ and Fayetteville, NC. In those cities, city counsel dictated police policy and interfered with police operations so much that those departments failed to maintain order, and in so doing failed the police officers and the people.[11] It was suggested that professional managers and commanders were not in control of those police departments (although they tried), but rather political agendas. Police personnel were highly regarded by the residents in Midland suggesting that most of the police officers, despite political interference (assuming this thought has merit), attempted to provide quality police service and enhance public safety even if it meant the loss of their job.

ENDNOTES

1. In conversations and observations with the Midland Police Department, Chamber of Commerce, Midland Websites, and newspapers, it appeared that a single culture influenced the control of Midland's population. In the study that follows which measured police performance conducted by the principle writer, the majority of the participants seemed to represent a different culture other than the predominant culture in Midland. See Midland's Website for more detail: http://www.ci.midland.tx.us/.

2. Source: Midland's Website: http://www.ci.midland.tx.us/

3. See US Census Website: http://factfinder.census.gov/. Actually, the population of Midland declined by 523 people or 5% in one year.

4. Midland's Website reports: http://www.ci.midland.tx.us/.

5. See Midland Police Department on-line at http://www.basinlink.com/mpd/.

6. See Sutham Cheurprakobkit (2000) from the University of Texas of the Permian Basin at Odessa. Data analysis was based on a telephone survey of 251 residents in Midland and Odessa, Texas.

7. See Cheurprakobkit and Bartsch, 1999.

8. See the Bureau of Justice Statistics. (1980). *The Hispanic Victim: Advance National Crime Survey Report.* And the Bureau of the Census. (1991). *The Hispanic population in the United States.* March 1990. Current Population Report, Series P-20 (455), and David L. Carter. (1985). Hispanic interaction with the criminal justice system in Texas: Experiences, attitudes, and performance. *Journal of Criminal Justice, 11,* 213–227.

9. Those areas included deployment of routine police auto, bike, and boat patrol, decisions on mini stations, building owner notification, use of police force, priorities of calls for service, police officer disciplinary actions, police training, and officer promotions.

10. This is when English and another language and only Spanish or Portuguese were added together.

11. See Stevens, D. J. (2001a). *Case studies in community policing* (p. 259). Upper Saddle River, NJ: Prentice Hall.

CHAPTER 9

TESTING POLICE PERFORMANCE IN PALM BEACH COUNTY, FLORIDA

INTRODUCTION

In 2001, Palm Beach County's population was approximately 1,200,000 with 45 new residents arriving daily. The county spreads over 2,386 square miles. To appreciate how large Palm Beach County is, it dwarfs Rhode Island and is larger than Delaware. There are 37 municipalities and numerous unincorporated areas in the county. The Supervisor of Elections Office in 1998 reported that there were almost 608,000 people registered to vote in Palm Beach County including around 276,000 registered Democrats, 229,000 registered Republicans, and 103,000 people registered as Independents or in other political parties. West Palm Beach is the largest among the County's 37 municipalities with almost 79,000 people.

The 1995 per-capita personal income in Palm Beach County was $34,497 as compared to a statewide per-capita income of $22,534. The Federal Department of Housing and Urban Development reported the median family income for 1999 was $55,600, and the property appraiser reported that the average price for a new home in Palm Beach County was $120,000 in 1997.

More than 240,000 cars and trucks travel through the county over Interstate 95 and the Florida Turnpike each day. Palm Beach International Airport serves an annual traveling public of more than 5,844,098. In 1998, 2,428,000 people visited Palm Beach County hotel facilities. The eastern edge of the county is known as Florida's "Gold Coast." Palm Beach County's 45 miles of shoreline was named "Gold Coast" after the gold recovered from the Spanish Galleons that sank offshore. Sugar is one of their county's largest agricultural crops, with 1,923,308 tons produced annually. The Palm Beach County Sheriff's Office continues an attempt to meet the needs of their diverse and rapidly growing communities.

PALM BEACH SHERIFF'S OFFICE

In 2001, the Palm Beach Sheriff's Office employed 2,736 personnel including 1,690 sworn officers and 1,046 civilians.[1] Of the sworn officers, 631 of them work in one of the county's jails. As of January 16, 2001, there were 2,258 housed inmates. Of those inmates, 747 were confined in Stockade, 1,400 at the Main Detention Center, and 111 were confined at Belle Glade.[2] In addition, there were 5,250 volunteers working in the county's communities. The Palm Beach Sheriff's Office Communications' Dispatchers handled 676,483 police and administrative calls for service during 1998.

CORE VALUES AND BELIEFS OF SHERIFF'S OFFICE

> We value above all our commitment of service to the community
>
> Integrity must not be compromised
>
> Honest relationships and trust are essential
>
> We respect each other in all activities and there will be no tolerance for discrimination of any kind
>
> We work together as a team for the betterment of the community and our agency
>
> We believe in helping our employees realize their full potential
>
> Efficiency means the difference between success and failure
>
> We will relentlessly pursue a more efficient way to do everything we undertake

The primary purpose of the Sheriff's Office is to preserve and ensure quality of life of all individuals and entities they serve. Their mission is to become the most efficient and effective Sheriff's Office in the State of Florida.

CRIME PREVENTION PROGRAMS

The Palm Beach Sheriff's Office Department of Law Enforcement engages in patrol activities and community related initiatives, and supervises investigative functions of the agency. It also operates the following programs:

- Crime Stoppers is a not-for-profit citizens' organization that provides monetary rewards to people who furnish crime-related information.
- Bicycle registration program provides a means of identifying bicycles to aid in bike theft deterrence.

- Citizen Observer Patrol is a volunteer effort to patrol the neighborhood. There are over 4,200 volunteers in the program.
- Operation CAT (Combat Auto Theft) is a voluntary program that identifies cars to be stopped between 1:00 a.m. and 5:00 a.m. Owners who are unlikely to be driving at that time may register their car so that if it is seen on the road during those hours, the driver's right to be in possession of the vehicle is challenged.
- The Eagle Academy is a program for at-risk juveniles.
- The Mounted COP Unity with 102 trained volunteers was developed.
- Palm Star Process serves as a catalyst for initiating improvements in service delivery.
- District VII was created to increase road patrol service to the south county area.
- Road Patrol deputies are assigned to specific neighborhoods. These officers shifted from simply taking reports to solving problems of the neighborhoods patrolled, but their first priority is to respond to emergency calls for service.
- Traffic Enforcement Unit consists of motorcycles, community service aids (CSA), and DUI enforcement officers. Officers are deployed based on an analysis of traffic crashes.
- Community Service Aids (CSA) consists of staff (not sworn) trained to respond to non-crime calls for service.
- Bicycle Patrol Unit has a variety of uses, from tactical deployment in high crime areas to educational awareness of bicycle safety.
- TRIAD of Palm Beach County was discussed in more detail in *Community Policing in the 21st Century.*

COMMUNITY POLICING UNIT (CPU)

Traditional policing methods of responding to calls for service, investigation of crime, and arrest of criminals had not reduced criminal activity, the agency announced several years ago. Therefore, the Sheriff's Office developed a District IV staff which works with the community to solve those issues through Problem Oriented Policing (POP). POP is a customized response to the particular needs of that neighborhood. Deputies are assigned to specific neighborhoods, and work with the community to solve the neighborhood problems. Community involvement is a daily mission. McGruff, the crime fighting dog, visits schools frequently, pumping paws with students.

THE COMMUNITY ACTION TEAM

The Community Action Team (CAT) is comprised of crime prevention and education officers who use problem-solving to assist the patrol districts in especially troublesome areas. CAT officers work in conjunction with patrol, as well as other units. Usually at the request of the Patrol District Commander, the team augments current patrol resources within a district in places where extra patrol and enforcement is needed. CAT also assists with special projects such as truancy sweeps, tobacco enforcement and gang graffiti documentation and eradication. CAT specializes in problem-solving in neighborhoods where normal patrol response is sometimes restrained by the mere volume of calls for service.

LOCAL STUDY

A local study examined the impact of community policing by analyzing citizens' perception of crime and police work before and after implementation of a community-oriented policing program in three neighborhoods in the city of West Palm Beach, Florida.[3] Results showed positive findings about community policing, including: perception of decreased local crime, increased perception of police performance, neighborhood improvement, and police-community relationship. Implications concerning the relationship between the community and the police, citizen satisfaction, and public services were discussed. Yet, while there appears to be some congruence between the local study's results and the investigation that follows, there are more differences than similarities.

PREPARING TO TEST THE ATTITUDES
OF COMMUNITY MEMBERS

In an attempt to measure the attitudes of residents living in Palm Beach County, one community was chosen due to its accessibility to Deputies Matt Lavigna and Steven Dickinson,[4] and due in part to its typical population as compared to other diverse communities in the county. That is, as could be expected, the single housing values of the county move from hundreds of millions of dollars per home to very low prices in the cities of Belle Galdes and Pohokee. Although the deputies knew that each county neighborhood was different and therefore a policing strategy that might work in one neighborhood might not work in another, they chose to survey a neighborhood that was more similar than not to the other communities in the county. Therefore, a concept home development was selected. Typically, a concept home is a home built in a development in Florida that was established for first-time home buyers who might have less money available for a down payment than the typical worker. The structures were new but sold unfinished in an attempt to keep prices low. It was expected that each buyer would, of course, finish his or her home in keeping with local zoning regulations.

In Palm Beach County there are approximately 7,200 residents living in 1,800 conceptual home developments. These developments were approximately 12 years old at the time of this study. In 2001, the once first-time homebuyers began selling or renting their homes in order to move into more affluent neighborhoods. Although this notion was applauded, as those residents moved from the neighborhoods new residents were less connected to the county and seemed to neglect their property, producing unpleasant responses from other older residents who then put their homes on the market. The concept home communities were drastically changing, and since the new residents seemed to come from more urban communities such as Miami, they were also more urban savvy individuals, many of whom accepted criminal activities as a way of life. This finding is consistent with information from Harris County Precinct 4 (Houston, TX), a similar county to Palm Beach in which an urbanized population moved to the county and with them came more serious criminal behavior.[5]

In the county, there were four concept home developments: Chestnut Hills, Brentwood Lakes, Indian Pines, and Lee's Crossing. Chestnut Hills was comprised of 198 homes that range in price from $90,000 to $120,000. Most residents were renters. There is a mixture of whites and Latinos in the community. Many of the surveys used in this study were distributed and collected by the deputies who conducted a door-to-door survey of the residents during the spring of 2001. Other surveys were completed by residents who attended community meetings, and others contacted the principle investigator after being contacted by the deputies.

TESTING POLICE PERFORMANCE
IN PALM BEACH COUNTY, FLORIDA

There were 155 surveys completed by residents of Palm Beach County who reported that they lived in Palm Beach County for an average of 8 years (see Table 9.1). Their average age was 45. Fifty-one (33%) of the residents surveyed characterized their employment as a blue-collar job and 39 (25%) as a white-collar job. Also, 18 (12%) were retired, 10 (7%) were students, 12 (8%) worked in retail, and 20 (13%) were small business owners. There were 95 (61%) female and 60 (39%) male respondents. Twenty-nine (19%) described themselves as white, 60 (39%) as black, 20 (13%) as Latino, 26 (17%) as Asian, and 20 (13%) ignored the question.

When the participants were asked what homeland best represented them, the majority reported it was the USA (85, 55%), 16 (10%) said China or Asia, 13 (8%) said Cape Verde or Cuba, 15 (10%) said Central or South America or Mexico, 4 (3%) Haiti, the Dominican Republic, or the Caribbean. Also, 9 (6%) reported Eastern Europe and 7 (5%) said Western Europe. One hundred and three (67%) said they spoke English at home, 20 (13%) spoke English and another language, 19 (12%) spoke only Spanish or Portuguese. Finally, 140 (90%) respondents reported they rented their home, and 12 (8%) were homeowners.

MAKING DECISIONS AND MEETINGS

Rarely did any participants report they were involved in any of the decision-making processes conducted by deputies.[6] In fact, only 6 (2%) of the sample reported that they were involved in some form of discussion with deputies about policing matters. Yet, 80 (52%) participants reported they were willing to participate in those discussions.

At community meetings, two-thirds of the participants reported that most or at least some of the time community members worked together. However, one in four reported that only sometimes were community residents encouraged to attend community police meetings. Also, 27 (17%) reported they left a meeting with a to-do list, and 23 (15%) reported they had helped develop their own problem solving remedies. At many meetings, while they revealed the deputies did not monopolize discussions with enforcement discussions, less often were previous problem solving plans changed to fit new findings. Overall, 110 (71%) said they were not sure if any of the solutions coming from problem solving discussions were practical. And, 7 (5%) said they were impractical solutions while 38 (25%) reported those solutions were practical.

CHANGES

When Palm Beach County survey takers were asked in what way their community was safer since the community started meeting (as opposed to the participant attending meetings), many comments were offered which fit the following categories:

- Response time of deputies was about the same: 60 (39%)
- People who previously remained quiet about crime now talked about it: 58 (37%)
- People now helped deputies do their job: 25 (16%)
- Didn't know or offered no comment: 11 (7%)

Finally, 65 (42%) said they didn't know how deputies contributed to their safety.

GREATEST NEIGHBORHOOD PROBLEMS

The 155 Palm Beach County participants reported their most serious community issue were:

- Streets, lights, empty buildings/houses, and graffiti
- Street drug activity
- Gangs and juveniles

TABLE 9.1 Characteristics of Palm Beach County, Florida Sample, N = 155

	NUMBERS	PERCENTS[*]/RANGE
Length of Time	8.1 years	1–31 years
Age	45	26–71
Occupation		
Blue Collar	51	33%
White Collar	39	25%
Retired	18	12%
Student	10	7%
Retail	12	8%
Business Owner	20	13%
Other/Missing	5	3%
Gender		
Females	95	61%
Males	60	39%
Race		
White	29	19%
Black	60	39%
Latino	20	13%
Asian	26	17%
Missing	20	13%
Homeland		
Western Europe	7	5%
Eastern Europe	9	6%
Haiti/Dominican/Caribbean	4	3%
Central/South America/Mexico	15	10%
Cape Verde/Cuba	13	8%
China/Asia	16	10%
USA	85	55%
Language Spoken Home		
English	103	67%
English and another language	20	13%
Only Spanish or Portuguese	19	12%
Other/Missing	13	9%
Residents		
Rented	140	90%
Owned	12	8%
Lived with others	3	2%

[*]All percents rounded. Missing cases not always included.

- Parking, traffic, and speeders
- Home invasion
- Fear or lack of trust of police
- Panhandlers and prostitutes

Specifically, 49 (32%) participants reported their most serious community problem related to streets, lights, empty buildings/houses, and graffiti,[7] and 27 (17%) reported it was street drug activity. These responses were followed by a three-way tie among gangs and juveniles; parking, traffic, and speeding; and home invasion— reported by 23 (15%) participants in each category. Finally, 7 (5%) participants reported fear or luck of trust of deputies, and 3 (2%) said panhandlers and prostitutes. Unleashed animals were also mentioned as a big problem in connection with the above answers.

REMEDIES

When the Palm Beach County participants were asked what should be done to curb those serious neighborhood problems, the following conceptual categories were suggested:

- Quality policing and municipal services
- Young supervision and enforced curfews
- Homeowners encouraged to stay in the neighborhood[8]

Sixty-two (40%) residents reported the best way to curb serious neighborhood problems was through quality policing and municipal services. Concerning the issue of policing, they recommended strict enforcement and punitive action toward violators, especially youths, reported 53 (34%) participants. For instance, participants wanted an increase in neighborhood patrols since they felt the sheriff's department was not providing adequate protection and the courts were not providing strict enough sanctions, especially among youths. However, patrols and sanctions did not apply to their youths, but youths and violators who lived elsewhere. Selective enforcement might be one way to describe their thoughts on this matter. Many participants said their youths should be closely supervised, especially during non-school hours, and that parents should be informed of curfew violations, but their children should not be taken into custody. Parent(s), they argued, should be advised of resident-violators. It was easy to get a sense that community members wanted more control over their children and wanted less official intrusion from a police agency.

However, patrols and sanctions were not the primary remedies. Participants wanted municipal services. Some of those services included garbage pickup, street repair, and of largest concern, secured abandoned homes in the area. Many offered another suggestion: remodel those abandoned properties and make them financially available to local residents since many of those residents rented "from banks." Several mentioned that they knew community members who would help rebuild those homes and that work could enhance family-neighborhood status. Those thoughts were linked to those who reported that residents should be encouraged to remain in the community (apparently, there was high homeowner turnover in the communities surveyed). However, this finding was part of a larger situation among the participants. One first impression could be that most of those individuals owned their homes, but a closer look revealed that many were making monthly and biweekly payments to banks and other lenders who originally foreclosed on those properties. Current occupants weren't owners at all but building towards ownership. That is, respondents were renting with an option to buy. Once an appropriate down payment and credit history were obtained, loans could be made. Recall that renters were overly represented in this sample. Furthermore, many of those owners, as it turned out, were more likely represented by female-headed households residing in a single family dwelling preparing for home ownership.

The community members polled revealed other thoughts that can be divided into two central themes:

- Oversight committees with results
- Police and other county departments work together

Seventy (45%) residents furthered their thoughts about solving neighborhood problems by arguing that the community should have influence and representation in county oversight by participating in police and city committees that dealt with issues such as hiring, services, discipline, and promotional issues. There was a thought weaved throughout their responses that they wanted to see immediate results. They were impatient with the Sheriff's Office and county services, suggesting there had been frequent policy changes from those agencies. Another thought that arose was if they didn't approve of current policy, they could wait until policy changed (which apparently happened often). The residents were often told of a change and it was promised, but it actually surfaced less frequently than suggested and never lasted long. Although only seven participants reported fear or a lack of trust of police, many participants made their position clear that they rejected both municipal and police policy as reflective of their community. That is, they appeared to be apathetic or tolerant toward county workers and its deputies. In the words of one participant, "when I see a deputy cruising around, I don't see him at all. They're invisible."

SAFETY

When participants were asked how safe it was to live in their neighborhood as compared to a year ago, 49 (32%) reported things were about the same. Nothing changed. However, 46 (30%) participants reported they felt safer than they had a year ago, but 36 (23%) also reported that they felt less safe.

POLICE PERFORMANCE RATED

Based on the experience a participant had with deputies:

- 94 (61%) rated police performance as professional
- 18 (12%) rated police performance as fair
- 4 (3%) rated police performance as frightening
- 39 (25%) missing

When deputies responded to a call for service, 76 (50%) said response time was excellent or good, 63 (41%) said officer(s) solved the problem, 83 (53%) reported officer(s) put them at ease, 91 (59%) reported officer(s) were helpful, and 107 (69%) reported officer(s) were dressed appropriately.

POLICE EFFECTIVENESS

When the participants were asked how effective the sheriff's office was in responding to neighborhood problems, findings revealed the sheriff's office was:

- Effective: 61 (39%)
- Ineffective: 54 (35%)
- Missing: 40 (26%)

What else did the respondents say? Almost nine of every ten of them thought deputies should spend more time making personal contact with neighborhood residents. Most everyone strongly agreed that deputies should be assigned to a neighborhood on a long-term basis, and there was a consensus that deputies should be more involved with school activities. Many survey takers thought deputies were polite and that deputies did not speak down to them. However, 51 (33%) said the police rarely listened to their non-criminal concerns. This thought is consistent with the 58 (37%) survey takers who felt uncomfortable in taking suggestions or complaints to the sheriff's office.

THE FUTURE

When the participants were asked about the future of their neighborhood a year from when the survey was taken, they said:

- A better place to live: 63 (41%)
- Will stay about the same: 49 (32%)
- A worse place to live: 23 (15%)
- Not sure about its future: 20 (13%)

SUMMARY

The characteristics of Palm Beach County were offered, followed by a description of the Palm Beach Sheriff's Office, including their history and their programs. The task of District IV personnel was discussed and it was explained they were involved with community matters which included escorting McGruff, their crime fighting dog, on visits to area schools. Also reviewed was the Community Action Team designed to operate from a problem-solving orientation. This team, it was revealed, concentrated efforts in targeted neighborhoods and often was deployed to aid other units. A local study was briefly discussed. Preparations were revealed to undertake an investigation of Palm Beach County with the aid of deputies from the Sheriff's office. Finally, the results from the investigation conducted in Palm Beach County were shared, which included their most serious neighborhood issues and their ideas about solving those concerns. Although active enforcement and strict punishment was recommended, it applied to outsiders as opposed to community residents. Deputy and agency performance were rated high and the future looked good for these residents.

CONCLUSION: PALM BEACH COUNTY, FLORIDA

Based on the evidence produced by 155 residents of Palm Beach County and the public records of both the county of Palm Beach and the Palm Beach Sheriff's Office, strides toward enhancing community police initiatives have been favorable. Reported crime was down, yet the fear of crime was high, and quality of life experiences are suspect. Although the conduct of deputies in general was rated as professional, the problem-solving solutions or policies of the sheriff's office were rated as ineffective. True, the sheriff's office had many excellent programs, but a uniform (and permanent) policy did not exist at the time of this investigation. Consequently, policy, programs, the way those programs were conducted, and their outcomes were unpredictable to the residents polled.

Community police strategies go beyond an agency just saying they have one. In this case, it appears to be more of a convenience to the sheriff's department than a preventative philosophy. Although the sheriff's office of Palm Beach appears to have good intentions, the evidence failed to show consistent problem-solving strategies even existed. For instance, the agency claimed it solved community problems through District IV personnel and their Community Action Teams. But, from the perspective of the community, few programs were centered in any systematic solving approach and fewer yet considered neighborhood issues (as opposed to sheriff issues). The county sheriff's program called Community Action Team allegedly operated from a problem-solving orientation, but the program, under the watchful command of top commanders, was only operated in targeted communities and during challenging situations. Accounts in cities such as Nashville, St. Petersburg, and Camden demonstrated targeting in challenged neighborhoods and/or specific events including announcements of the residence of a sexual offender can heighten the frustration levels of residents and maximize their fear of crime.[9] Life experiences change due to fear levels of a community.[10] Also, many residents viewed police targeting as another way to bolster police power.[11]

One result is probably uncertainty from the community members impacted and from the deputies who conducted those programs. Uncertainty can lead to unstableness, public disorder, and mistrust. This thought was evident in the reports of the participants as they revealed their lack of confidence in policy of both county services and the services provided by the sheriff's office. The bottom line is the community members polled felt unsafe and uncertain in their own neighborhoods and next year things were likely to be unchanged.

When individuals feel an imbalance with their social environment due to an unstableness, a lack of control, and/or an inability to predict outcomes, those individuals are likely to have different life experiences than others who may not experience any of those dynamics. Since the participants were not surveyed before community police initiatives arrived in their county, it is hard to tell how their life experiences have changed. Nonetheless, if there were evidence suggesting that their life experiences were different due in part to the dynamics mentioned, it could be argued with a great deal of confidence that it creates dissonance, an unpleasant state of arousal. Maybe this thought can help to explain Midland and Sacramento's situation, too. Nonetheless, cognitive dissonance is centered on the idea that most of us do what we must to establish internal consistency and balance in our lives. When behavior does not match attitudes, for example, we often change our attitude to match behavior. Furthermore, individuals in dissonance will discount information about results produced from their conduct, alter logical information that explains those results, and often rationalize their motives about their conduct.

Therefore, to answer the primary question under investigation: does police practice enhance neighborhood safety issues and provide social order or stability? Perhaps the best answer is no, not entirely. Also, it was believed prior to the investigation that community police strategies gave rise to crime control, reduced the fear of crime, and enhanced resident quality of life experiences. That thought was not supported by the data.

Also, there was little evidence that any of the community members engaged in police decision-making processes in Palm Beach County. True, while some of residents attended meetings, there was little evidence of any of them influencing police or county decision-making processes at any level.

One recommendation concerning policing strategies is to develop and implement an agency-wide philosophy guided through a partnership with neighborhood members (which must include empowerment and training of community officers and community members) and county agencies to better serve Palm Beach County.[12] Second, appropriate communication and training of all county personnel and community members within the partnership is one way to guarantee success. Policing is no longer a secret enterprise nor is it expected to function alone in controlling crime, reducing the fear of crime, and enhancing quality of life issues. Third, develop and implement a SARA type problem-solving system to be utilized jurisdiction wide. Fourth, since problem-solving activity is a shared responsibility, community members must be accountable and equally responsible for developing, maintaining, and following through on remedies to resolve neighborhood issues.

However, lest we forget, low grades were given to county services, too. Of the participants' top three most serious neighborhood issues, two had less to do with primary functions of the sheriff's office. What's happening in part is that with inconsistent community initiatives and a lack of a county-wide philosophy, personal feelings about safety are affected. Specifically, fear levels have increased in Palm Beach County among community members who live in those conceptual home developments.

The sheriff's office has its own internal problems that may march to a different drummer than partnering with community members. Added to their own agenda appears to be a county that provides inadequate services to constituents who are located within a lower socio-economic class than others residents. There is little doubt in the minds of the many residents that people who live in the two million dollar homes in Palm Beach County are in short supply of municipal services not that they need street lights. One guess is that lower class residents of Palm Beach County get municipal crumbs and less attention in comparison, but more police enforcement. Evidence to support this perspective lies with the fact that their Community Action Team (CAT) officers work in conjunction with patrol and assist with enforcement. And all of their preventive programs are directed through an enforcement division commander and are targeted at conceptual home developments. The sheriff's office has an excellent opportunity to play a leadership role in guiding municipal services to enhance the constituents of the county.

However, consider that the county sheriff's department has many diverse constituents, many miles to cover, and probably few resources. Equally important, many of their constituents are transplants from elsewhere which can mean that their individual investment in the community is less than people who might have called the area home or their birthplace. Community members can help or hinder the community partnership experience. Additionally, the sheriff's office is but one county agency, but the most visible and therefore they get the heat.

ENDNOTES

1. See Palm Beach County Sheriff's Office Website at http://www.pbso.org/.

2. Jail capacity is 2,891 total of which 967 could be housed at the Stockade, 1,798 at Main, and 126 at Belle.

3. For more detail see Liou, T. K., & Savage, E. G. (1996). Citizen perception of community policing impact. *Public Administration and Management: An Interactive Journal, 1*(1). [Online], Available at http://www.pamij.com/liou1.html.

4. Without the aid of Deputy Steve Dickinson, measuring the attitudes of the community members of Chestnut Hills would have been impossible.

5. See Dennis J. Stevens (2001a). *Case studies in community policing*. (pp. 147–165). Upper Saddle River, NJ: Prentice Hall.

6. Those areas included deployment of routine police auto, bike, and boat patrol, decisions on mini stations, building owner notification, use of police force, priorities of calls for service, police officer disciplinary actions, police training, and officer promotions.

7. Note: concerning these participants' most serious problem, of all the jurisdictions investigated this is the only jurisdiction where the participants reported abandoned homes instead of abandoned buildings as their most serious problem.

8. In one respect, the response of these 15 participants was different from those in the combined study who described home ownership opportunities.

9. For more details see Zevitz, R. G., & M. A. Farkas. (2000, December). Sex offender community notification: Assessing the impact in Wisconsin. National Institute of Justice: Research in Brief. NCJ 179992. [On-line]. Available: http://www.ojp.usdoj.gov/nij and Dennis J. Stevens. (1999d, March). Police tactical units and community response. *Law and Order, 47*(3), 48–52.

10. For more detail, see Dennis J. Stevens. (1998b). Urban communities and homicide: Why American blacks resort to murder. *Police and Society, 8,* 253–267. And (1998c). Incarcerated women, crime, and drug addiction. *The Criminologist, 22*(1), 3–14.

11. For more detail, see Dennis J. Stevens. (2001a). *Case studies in community policing*. (pp. 61–89, 228–250). Upper Saddle River, NJ: Prentice Hall.

12. Personal note: Recommendations can come easy when the principal researcher lives 1,500 miles away.

CHAPTER 10

TESTING POLICE PERFORMANCE IN SACRAMENTO, CALIFORNIA

INTRODUCTION

The Maidu Indians, a branch of the Valley Nisenan group, lived in Sacramento before the Anglo invasion.[1] Sacramento is located at the junction of two rivers, the Sacramento and the American. It is surrounded on the south by the delta, to the east by the foothills of the Sierra, and on the north and west by farms. Sacramento was named in 1808 by Gabriel Moraga, a Spanish explorer who named the valley for the Holy Sacrament, a Christian religious rite.

In the winter of 1848, James Marshall built a water powered sawmill 45 miles up the south fork of the American River at a place called Coloma for his employer, John Sutter. Yet, on the morning of January 24, 1848, Marshall reached into the icy waters and found gold. Needless to say, "Gold Fever" was felt worldwide.

Gold fever created the largest peacetime migration in history. People from around the globe came to California in search of their dreams. While the Gold Rush brought wealth to many of Sacramento's early citizens, it also brought brawls, gunfights, and robberies.

Today, as the oldest incorporated city in California, its state capital, and home of California State University, Sacramento has enjoyed over 150 years of history which is rich in cultural, religious, ethnic, and economic growth. US Census reports that in 2000, there were 407,018 people living in approximately 98 square miles of which 196,549 (48%) were white, 62,968 (16%) were black or African American, 67,635 (17%) were native Hawaiian and Pacific Islanders, and 87,974 (22%) were Hispanic or Latino (of any race).

THE SACRAMENTO POLICE DEPARTMENT (SPD)

The SPD consists of 642 sworn officers (548 males, 94 females), 376 full-time civilians, 129 part-time civilians, and 107 volunteers.[2] During the calendar year of 1998

139

the SPD logged 385,085 calls for service and 25,706 arrests including misdemeanor cites.[3]

The chief's statement follows:

> The Sacramento Police Department is working to make the City of Sacramento a safe place to live and work by forming partnerships with its citizens and businesses. To us, providing Police services is a lot more than just writing a crime report after a crime has occurred; it means working with the community to prevent crime and to solve community problems. I invite you to become our partners in making your neighborhood a better place to live. Being a partner might mean:
>
> - Participating in a neighborhood watch group or neighborhood improvement committee
> - Volunteering at a neighborhood school or youth organization
> - Staying informed and getting involved in community issues that matter to you
> - Being an observant, caring and considerate neighbor
> - Volunteering with the Police Department
>
> Please join us!
>
> Sincerely,
>
> Arturo Venegas, Jr. Chief of Police[4] (March, 2001)

Mission Statement: The mission of the SPD is to work in partnership with the community to protect life and property, solve neighborhood problems and enhance the quality of life in our City.

The SPD is divided into four sections: Technical Services, Investigations, Operations, and Office of the Chief. Their organizational chart reports that SPD's Neighborhood Policing and Problem Oriented Policing units are linked to Operations or deployment units (enforcement units) within the department. The SPD's community policing programs are under the command of a deputy chief who reports to the chief of police. Many of the programs offered by the SPD follow:

- Community Chaplaincy Program
- Citizens Academy
- Drug Free Zones
- Total Quality Management
- Expanded Problem Oriented Policing
- Decentralization of Office of Investigations
- Safe Streets
- Departmental Volunteer Program
- Business Problem Management Program
- Partners in Prevention
- Expressions Program
- Problem Identification and Conflict Resolution
- People Reaching Out

- Police Cadet Program
- Drug Abuse Education in the Workplace
- Drug Abuse Education Program
- Neighborhood Improvement Plan
- Neighborhood Reclamation
- Apartment Problem Management Program
- Property Management Assistance
- Crime Alert Program
- Magnet School Program
- InfoCom
- Police Reserve Officer Program
- Sacramento Police Athletic League

NEIGHBORHOOD ASSOCIATIONS

Within the city of Sacramento, there are 4 areas which contain approximately 90 neighborhood associations.[5] These associations have regular meetings that are attended by neighborhood residents who often discuss community matters. As opposed to showing all of the associations, a sample from Area 1 follows:

Boulevard Park Neighborhood Association

Campus Commons Park Corporation

College Glen Neighborhood Association

Downtown Neighborhood Association

East Sacramento Improvement Association

Fremont Park Neighborhood Association

Friends of H Street

Friendship Park Neighborhood Association

Mansion Flat Neighborhood Association

Marshall School Neighborhood Association

McKinley Elvas Neighborhood Alliance

Nepenthe Association

New Era Park Neighborhood Association

River Park Neighborhood Association

Sierra Oaks Neighborhood Association

Somerset Parkside Homeowners Association

Southside Park Neighborhood Improvement Association

Southside Park Neighborhood Association

Stanford Park Home Owners Association

Sutter Place Home Owners Association

The Neighborhood

Washington Park Neighborhood Improvement Association

West-Midtown Neighborhood Association

Winn Park Capitol Ave. Neighborhood Association

Each association is individually listed on-line along with information should someone wish to contact them.[6] For example, the Website for this association provides the following contact information about this group:

MANSION FLAT NEIGHBORHOOD ASSOCIATION
1509 G Street
Sacramento, CA 95814
(916) 442-6711, (916) 785-3189 (Day)
E-mail: t_souder@hotmail.com
Contact Person: Todd Souder

- Alternate Contact Person: Alica Wenbourne
  1509 F Street, Sacramento, 95814
  Phone (916) 443-7322, e-mail: alicia@mansionflats.org

- Council District: 1
- Association Boundaries:
  - North - C Street
  - South - J Street
  - East - 16th Street
  - West - 12th Street
- Criteria for Joining: Reside, own property or a business within the boundaries.

You can also contact this group at the Mansion Flats Web Page.

As we examine the Website closer, you might be tempted to click on the Mansion Flats Web Page. What you will find is another menu leading you to more information such as:

A Brief Association History

The Mansion Flats Neighborhood Association was founded in the Spring of 1991. As with most Associations, its founding was a reaction to the common problems confronting inner-city neighborhoods across this country in the decades of the 80's and 90's.

The old Washington Preservation District had been sliced by the major thoroughfares of 12th and 16th Streets. The residents between those streets became an "island" forgotten by the City of Sacramento—not a Redevelopment Area and not the up and coming "Midtown."

In an effort to enhance its "sense of place" the residents renamed the area "Mansion Flats" and began their Association and the hard task of reweaving the fabric of their tattered neighborhood.

In 1992, Mansion Flats (along with Alkali Flat) was proud to be chosen by the Sacramento Police Department for the City's first "Community Oriented Policing" project.

Mansion Flats was a member of the City's first "Area Teams" made up of Community Leaders, Planning, Code Enforcement, and Law Enforcement, the forerunner of the Neighborhoods, Planning & Development Services Department with four areas.

It is through these associations that community policing initiatives, as evidenced by the comments in Mansion Flats's description, are employed by the SPD. Although, there are other associations and partnerships that are not shown among those Web pages.

COMMUNITY POLICE INITIATIVES

When the SPD planned its community policing initiatives, commanders and officers alike were torn between two approaches: specialty or community policing programs versus a generalist approach to community policing.[7] Specifically, designated officers were assigned to specific units such as Neighborhood Police Officers, Bicycle Beat Officers, Neighborhood Policing Teams, Neighborhood Abatement Teams, Crime Prevention Patrol Units, and community oriented policing (COP) Officers. The generalist approach related to all SPD officers shared a role in community policing.

The SPD practiced various patrol strategies for all neighborhoods and mingled community policing initiatives with those strategies. With the availability of community policing grants and through the implementation of community policing strategies over the latter 1990s, many departments including the SPD moved forward in a direction of adapting some form of community policing. For SPD, they attempted to institutionalize it in the sense that it became the best option to deliver police service. Therefore, the official position of the SPD was traditional methods of policing were necessary but successful institutionalization of community policing concepts were seen as the department's way of doing business or what was referred to as the "right thing to do." The process of adapting a community approach to policing included an incorporation of community policing concepts from hiring to the promotion process. As in most police departments, personnel resisted this change, but the SPD felt that their officers accepted it more readily than in other departments.

OPPORTUNITY

The SPD felt empowerment guidelines had to be developed to create consistency as to how police personnel operate. That is many line officers had to possess the authority to make decisions that could aid the community. Implementation was a start, but institutionalizing community oriented policing (COP) initiatives was the long term objective. Basic training, field training program, and patrol services presented opportunities to learn and practice the principles of COP. Yet, ongoing training programs for in-service officers and civilian support staff were recognized as an essential step in this objective. Also, the role of support personnel in helping solve problems offered the opportunity to understand the importance of this process. The SPD mobilized their community members in a similar fashion as their officers and felt that it was equally important to recognize the resources that were available both internally and externally.

Team building and liaison with resource agencies was emphasized. Once the orientation to COP was developed in the community and within local government, accountability for resolving problems became efficient, and more individuals aided in the process. For instance, in 1998, the City Council authorized the Police Blue Ribbon Committee to investigate and recommend "changes in processing and investigating citizen complaints of police misconduct and in deployment of police vehicles in emergency response or pursuit modes."[8]

One result of that committee's investigation was a recommendation of a new unit, The Police Monitor (PM), a civilian review of citizen complaints against officers. It was headed by a senior level appointee, who reported to the City Manager. The PM would have broad oversight powers to review both ongoing and completed investigations of citizen complaints and to encourage procedural and systemic reforms on behalf of the City Manager.

In 1997–1998 the PM committee reviewed 219 complaints against Sacramento police officers pursuant to alleged improper conduct. Of that number, 65 reported officers used unnecessary force, 27 reported improper action or procedure, 9 reported discrimination, and 118 were comprised of "other" alleged infractions. Most of those complaints were against white officers (these officers consisted of 71% of the sworn officers of the SPD at that time) especially those with three years of experience of less. Of the total complaints filed in one calendar year: 43% were African Americans, 21% were white, 9% were Hispanic, 1% were Asian, 3% other, and 23% decided not to give their race.

When resident complaints from other cities in California of similar size (both population and sworn officers) as Sacramento were compared,[9] the following information was learned. Oakland processed 307 complaints, Long Beach 119, and Fresno processed 68 complaints; however, Fresno does not have a method or a committee to review complaints. On the subject of unnecessary force or the intentional discharge of police weapons hitting citizens, Sacramento reported 6, Oakland reported 9, Long Beach 4, and Fresno 16 (of which 10 offenders were not hit) (based on January to July, 2000). Therefore, Sacramento took pride in their lower complaint statistics and officer involved shootings and argued that PM was in part responsible.

The Blue Ribbon Committee also recommended significantly enhanced driver training and evaluation for officers, and clarification and elaboration of vehicle pursuit and response policy. It urged the SPD to revise its vehicle pursuit policy to prohibit hot pursuits of individuals for minor violations or infractions and perhaps stolen vehicles.

The creation of the Office of Police Accountability (OPA) was also developed as a result of that commission. Its responsibilities, among other things, were to act as the city's cultural diversity change team, champion citywide and department efforts, steer senior management in leading these cases, and act as the voice of the people not heard. One of the primary goals of the OPA is to reach out to the community. Additionally, the Police Blue Ribbon Committee was responsible for:

- Developing an employee diversity program
- Defining a strategy for creating a more inclusive and high-performing culture
- Implementing this strategy
- Creating a change plan and process of the change plan
- Providing networking and visibility opportunities
- Supporting organization policies and practices that promote diversity and inclusion

PARTNERSHIPS

The SPD moved into partnerships that included agencies and organizations rather than community membership groups. These partnerships became the rule rather than the exception for the SPD.

For instance, the Regional Community Policing Institute (RCPI) was a Sacramento formed partnership with the California Attorney General's Office, the Commission on Peace Officers Standards and Training (POST), and the Sacramento County Alliance of Neighborhoods (SCAN).

Other professional partners included:

- The Attorney General's Crime and Violence Prevention Center established a statewide clearinghouse of Community Oriented Policing and Problem Solving (COPPS) information which is available to law enforcement and other government agencies, community groups, schools, and citizens through various mediums including telephone, fax and the Internet.
- POST has certified the training provided by RCPI and is handling travel and training reimbursements for workshop attendees. POST is also collaborating on the COPPS clearinghouse.
- Sacramento Country Alliance of Neighborhoods (SCAN) serves as a liaison between neighborhoods and local government. SCAN maintains communication between neighborhoods and helps to establish and monitor programs which will benefit residents. SCAN provides a link to enhance the community policing partnership throughout Sacramento. A Community Partnership for Safety Forum will be co-sponsored by RCPI and SCAN in 1999.

One partnership was with the California State University Police (CSUP)[10] at the California State University Sacramento.[11] In 1995, Sacramento received funding from a "COPPS More" grant and part of the funding was for a Neighborhood Police Officer (NPO) for the East Sacramento area where the university is located. The SPD and CSUP formed a partnership to provide community policing initiatives in the residential area that surrounds the campus. As a result, the CSUP officers engaged in community policing became a full-time member of SPD's central problem-oriented policing and NPO team. The CSUP officer uses SPD's facilities including its locker room, and drives an SPD patrol car. This relationship was a benefit to the CSUP and SPD in that the lines of communication between the two agencies were streamlined producing an immediate response and resources to critical incidents or major events that occurred on campus and in East Sacramento. The benefit for the SPD was resources available from the university such as student interns and assistance with studies such as this one.

STRATEGIC GOALS FOR YEARS 1994–2003

The SPD developed the following abbreviated list of strategic goals as new initiatives to:

1. Educate citizens as crime fighters
2. Develop a Citizen Police Academy
3. Increase participation in neighborhood watch and other crime prevention efforts
4. Work in partnership with the entire community to resolve crime-related problems
5. Assist the community in establishing drug free zones in targeted areas
6. Expand use of problem-oriented policing strategies throughout the department
7. Decentralize two area command structures into four command structures
8. Encourage community mobilization efforts through coordination
9. Solicit total community input through the continued use of community forums

CRIME RATES

As a matter of interest, when comparing crime rates with cities similar in size to Sacramento, it appears that Sacramento's Total Crime Index tends to be lower than most other cities its size.[12]

Both Cincinnati and Tulsa had lower motor vehicle theft than Sacramento (Cincinnati 1,822; Tulsa 3,711; Sacramento 6,260). Both Cincinnati and Tulsa reported more rapes and more aggravated assaults than Sacramento. Lastly, when reviewing Sacramento with other cities of similar size in California, both Fresno and Oakland reported more crime than Sacramento.

Also, as a matter of review, a year to year comparison of crime in Sacramento is compared from 1994 to 1999 in Sacramento (see Table 10.2). Crimes of personal

TABLE 10.1   Comparison of Total Crime Index among Similar Sized Cities

CITY	TOTAL CRIME INDEX
Alexandria, VA	47,923
Atlanta, GA	58,591
Cincinnati, OH	27,455
Fresno, CA	37,623
Miami, FL	50,259
Oakland, CA	38,048
Sacramento, CA	34,132
Tulsa, OK	28,517

violence (murder and forcible rape) seem to be up from 1998 to 1999, and nonviolent crimes against persons seem to be down.

The SPD moved in a direction of empowered partnerships, yet those partnerships are with other justice agencies more often than with the community. SPD may well have a rich community policing philosophy infused in each division, unit, program, and process within the department and its constituents aid in police decisions especially through the Office of Police Accountability. Yet, is the SPD a vision of a community policing success story? Measuring police performance should tell us more about their efforts.

TABLE 10.2   Uniform Crime Report

				AGGRA-			**MOTOR**
	MURDER	**FORCIBLE**	**ROBBERY**	**VATED**	**BURG-**	**LARCENY-**	**VEHICLE**
		RAPE		**ASSAULT**	**LARY**	**THEFT**	**THEFT**
1994	62	174	2,292	2,170	8,076	18,598	8,846
1995	57	158	2,129	1,936	8,003	18,538	7,982
1996	43	154	1,874	1,636	7,148	16,842	6,083
1997	41	161	1,851	1,664	6,873	17,282	6,260
1998	31	141	1,689	1,515	6,495	15,725	6,003
1999	56	143	1,450	1,438	4,805	14,761	4,460
% Change: '98 to '99	+80.6%	+1.4%	−14.1%	−5.1%	−26.0%	−6.1%	−25.7%
% Change '94 to '99	−9.7%	−17.8%	−36.7%	−33.7%	−40.5%	−20.6%	−49.6%

Produced by The Crime Analysis Unit, Sacramento Police Department.

TESTING POLICE PERFORMANCE
IN SACRAMENTO, CALIFORNIA

There were 105 surveys completed by residents of Sacramento, California. They said that they lived in Sacramento for an average of 11 years (see Table 10.3). Their average age was 44. None of the participants characterized their employment as a blue-collar occupation, 4 (4%) described white-collar duties, 4 (4%) were retired, 1 was a student, 5 (5%) were retailers, 7 (7%) were business owners, and 84 (80%) left this question blank. The occupational responses were unexpected and cannot be satisfactorily explained. One thought is that many of the participants were students at the university and if that was the case, many of those students were non-traditionally aged university students since frequency tables indicated only 16 respondents were under the age of 31.

There were 60 (57%) female and 42 (40%) male respondents. Largely, 17 (16%) described themselves as white, 27 (26%) as black, 18 (17%) as Latino, 19 (18%) as Asian, and 24 (23%) ignored the question.

When participants were asked about what homeland they recognized as theirs, 33 (31%) reported it was Western Europe, and 38 (36%) said Haiti, the Dominican Republic, or the Caribbean. Fifteen (14%) said Central or South America or Mexico, 12 (11%) China or Asia, and 7 (7%) reported it was the USA.

Concerning languages spoken at home, 35 (33%) spoke English at home, 29 (28%) spoke English and another language. Also, 35 (37%) spoke only Spanish or Portuguese at home. Finally, 8 (8%) said they rented, 91 (87%) said they owned their home, and 6 (6%) lived at home with parents or others.

MAKING DECISIONS AND MEETINGS

Twenty-three (22%) said they aided police in a decision-making process concerning routine police auto patrol, and 12 (12%) respondents said they aided the police with decisions about 911 priority calls. However, approximately one-third of the participants reported they would participate in police decision-making processes.

At community meetings, 34 (32%) said participants reported they sometimes worked together with other community members, but 33 (31%) reported they seldom or never worked together. Although 28 (27%) participants reported neighborhood residents were sometimes encouraged to attend community meetings, 33 (32%) said they were seldom or never encouraged to come to meetings. But, 54 (51%) participants left a meeting with a to-do list. Also, during those encounters or meetings, only 22 (21%) said they often developed their own problem-solving remedies.

At many meetings, 63 (60%) revealed the police monopolized conversations with enforcement discussions, but less than often were previous problem-solving plans changed to fit new findings. Yet, 78 (74%) said they were sure the solutions coming from problem-solving discussions were impractical.

CHANGES

When the Sacramento survey takers were asked in what way their community was safer since the community started meeting (as opposed to the participant attending meetings), many comments were offered which fit the following categories:

- Response time of officers was about the same: 12 (11%)
- Officers seemed to take an identity from the neighborhood: 47 (45%)
- People now helped the police do their job: 37 (35%)

And, 57 (54%) reported they were not sure how the Sacramento police contributed to their safety, but 37 (35%) said the police were more visible.

GREATEST NEIGHBORHOOD PROBLEMS

The 105 participants in Sacramento described their greatest neighborhood problem as:

- Streets, lights, empty buildings, and graffiti
- Fear or lack of trust of police
- No problem or others
- Street drug activity
- Panhandlers and prostitutes

Specifically, 29 (28%) reported their most serious neighborhood problem was centered in environmental conditions such as streets, lights, empty buildings, and graffiti issues. "If we have so much to be thankful for, then why are buildings empty and street lights dark?" one respondent wrote.

Also, 27 (26%) described a fear or lack of trust of the Sacramento police. In this case, it appeared that most of the participants characterized a lack of confidence in the department as opposed to a fear of the department. This finding is consistent only with the Boston sample while in the other jurisdictions, the participants referred to fear. For instance, several responses written in both English and Spanish typified numerous descriptions that talked about uncertainty of police service. Participants saw no link between police, family matters, neighborhood affairs, or crime. The problems of the family and the neighborhood were best left to those who could solve them, and that was not the police of Sacramento, they argued. In Boston, the lack of confidence had to do with the department changing policy often.

Twenty-two (21%) respondents insisted there wasn't any problem, at least there wasn't any that those individuals wanted to share with anyone. Thirteen (12%) reported street drug activity, and 9 (4%) saw the problems of the neighborhood as panhandlers and prostitutes.

REMEDIES

When 105 residents in Sacramento were asked how to curb neighborhood problems, they described primarily:

- Homeownership and business investment
- Municipal services

Forty-eight (46%) residents described the best way to solve neighborhood issues was through homeownership and business investment. It could be said that apparently there were so many homeowners living in substandard environmental conditions that maintenance of their community had much to do with their sense of pride. Trying to feel safe in your own home with little confidence in the police, with poor street lights, empty buildings, and graffiti everywhere, might be a signal to criminals and police alike that the neighborhood is prime for exploitation. This sounds like the classic description of the broken window's perspective. But, maybe it is also a signal about the people who live in poor conditions that accept the responsibility of those conditions. That is, they blame, and/or feel as though they too are "broken" in some way. Certainly, if this is the case, feelings of frustration and anger would follow. Also, 36 (34%) participants left this question blank supporting the notion that many felt uncomfortable with any answer.

The community members polled revealed other thoughts that can be divided into two central themes:

- Police and city oversight committees
- Political involvement

Eighty-six (82%) characterized the best way to solve their greatest neighborhood problems was through participation on police and city oversight committees. An influencing factor moving participants toward this conceptual category might be consistent with their ideas that streets, lights, and buildings needed maintenance and the confidence in police needed to be enhanced. Since these participants saw the police as government representatives (as did most of the participants in this investigation), to them it all meant the same—police were the government. Oversight committees included influence over city services. However, these participants did not want to aid in the decision-making processes of policing and city services, they wanted to be heard. There are many indicators that this sample was under the impression city

TABLE 10.3   Characteristics of Sacramento, California Sample, N = 105

	NUMBERS	PERCENTS[*]/RANGE
Length of Time	11 years	0–40 years
Age	44	19–75
Occupation		
Blue Collar	0	0%
White Collar	4	4%
Retired	4	4%
Student	1	1%
Retail	5	5%
Business Owner	7	7%
Other/Missing	84	80%
Gender		
Females	60	57%
Males	42	40%
Race		
White	17	16%
Black	27	26%
Latino	18	17%
Asian	19	18%
Missing	24	23%
Homeland		
Western Europe	33	31%
Eastern Europe	0	0%
Haiti/Dominican/Caribbean	38	36%
Central/South America/Mexico	15	14%
Cape Verde/Cuba	0	0%
China/Asia	12	11%
USA	7	7%
Language Spoken Home		
English	35	33%
English and another language	29	28%
Only Spanish or Portuguese	35	33%
Other/Missing	6	6%
Residents		
Rented	8	8%
Owned	91	87%
Lived with others	6	6%

[*]All percents rounded. Missing cases not always included.

government would "do the right thing" once their voices were heard. Continuing along this line of reasoning for the Sacramento sample, 12 (11%) thought political involvement was an answer to neighborhood problems, but again it must be clarified that involvement meant to be heard, expecting that their leaders would make decisions in their best interests. Their leaders weren't at fault for the poor conditions, the residents were! Or at least that's the impression they gave through their comments.

SAFETY

When the participants were asked how safe it was to live in their neighborhood as compared to a year ago, 40 (38%) said it was very unsafe, and 34 (32%) said nothing had changed. Twenty-eight (27%) said it was safer in their neighborhood as compared to last year, but only 3 (3%) said it was much safer.

POLICE PERFORMANCE RATED

Based on the experience a participant had with police:

- 44 (42%) rated police performance as professional
- 32 (31%) rated police performance as fair
- 21 (20%) rated police performance as frightening and/or intimidating

Also, when they commented on the performance of officers at a crime or an accident scene, 62 (59%) said response time was good or excellent, 48 (46%) said officer(s) solved the problem, 63 (60%) said officer(s) put them at ease, 52 (50%) said officer(s) were helpful, and only 38 (36%) said officer(s) were dressed appropriately. In each case, approximately 18% ignored the question.

POLICE EFFECTIVENESS

When participants were asked how effective the SPD was in responding to neighborhood problems, findings revealed the police agency was:

- Effective or very effective: 35 (17%)
- Ineffective: 86 (41%)
- Didn't know: 19 (9%)
- Police had their own agenda: 23 (11%)

What else did the respondents think? Almost all of them thought that specific officers should spend more time making personal contact with neighborhood residents, and they should be assigned to a neighborhood on a long-term basis. But, 53 (51%) thought the police talked down to them, however, they did think the Sacramento police listened to their non-criminal concerns. But, one-third of them said they were uncomfortable in taking their suggestions or complaints to the police.

THE FUTURE

When the participants were asked about the future, they reported the neighborhood a year from now would be:

- A better place to live: 0 (0%)
- It would stay about the same: 40 (38%)
- It would become a worse place to live: 30 (29%)
- Not sure about its future: 35 (33%)

It appears that many of the survey takers thought the future of Sacramento would not change and the chances of Sacramento becoming a worse place to live were likely.

SUMMARY

The city and police history were explored, and the chief made a statement about forming partnerships. A number of police programs were identified, along with community policing initiatives and opportunities that included blue ribbon panels that aided police strategies. The department's strategic goals, crime rates, and UCR comparisons were offered. When measuring police performance, findings revealed that over 80% of the participants did not indicate their occupation and that race was somewhat evenly divided between the four categories. The sample consisted of more women than men, and more individuals selected as a homeland Haiti, Dominican Republic, Caribbean, West Europe, or Central/South America or Mexico more often than the USA. A third of the sample spoke only Spanish or Portuguese at home and a high percent spoke two languages at home. Streets, lights, empty buildings, and graffiti along with a fear or lack of trust of police led the list of serious neighborhood problems. Solutions included home ownership and business investment, but both solutions were linked to the poor environmental condition of the community. While some participants rated individual officers with high marks concerning their professionalism, many more reported the police department was ineffective as opposed to effective in resolving community problems. Few thought their community would be a better place to live in the future.

CONCLUSION: SACRAMENTO, CALIFORNIA

Based on the evidence provided by 105 residents of Sacramento and the public records of both the city of Sacramento and the Sacramento Police Department, it appears that organizationally the SPD has advanced. But crime does not appear to be controlled in keeping with the explanations of the police agency and the fear of crime has increased as compared to the previous year. Therefore, it is safe to argue the quality of life experiences for Sacramento residents doesn't seem to be at expected levels. In short, to answer the primary question under investigation: does police practice enhance neighborhood safety issues and provide social order or stability? It would appear that police practice has little to do with social order or stability in Sacramento. Also, it was believed before the investigation that community police strategies gave rise to crime control, reduced the fear of crime, and enhanced resident quality of life experiences. The data do not support that perspective.

Many community members attended meetings, but there is little evidence that any of them influenced police decision-making processes. In support of this conclusion, based on the information given to the principal investigator, it was the department that developed the strategic goals for 1994–2003 as opposed to partnership with the community. It is also curious that the SPD empowered line officers to assist community members in developing solutions for neighborhood problems, but community members held no official power to further their ideas. That could imply they were merely observers at those meetings. It is true that when the Police Monitor (PM) was established, a civilian reviewed complaints against officers. The PM had broad oversight powers to review both ongoing and completed investigations of citizen complaints and to encourage procedural and systemic reforms on behalf of the City Manager. But that position was filled by a senior level appointee who also reported to the city manager.

Furthermore, it was hoped that the more culturally diverse members influenced the decisions of the police the greater the likelihood that public order will be enhanced. There was little evidence to support the idea that community members regardless of their cultural diversity influenced any police decisions, therefore public order was not necessarily enhanced in Sacramento as a result of community policing initiatives. For instance, the Office of Police Accountability (OPA) was to act as the city's cultural diversity change team, champion citywide and department efforts, steer senior management in leading these cases, and act as the voice of the people not heard. Their primary goal was to reach the community. However, its organizational structure and chain of command was similar to the Police Monitor. Typical community members were not involved with official policy at any level.

One impression that was developed through a review of all the descriptions offered by the participants about their most serious neighborhood issues was that a neighborhood with poor streets and lighting, empty buildings, and graffiti demonstrates that the city doesn't care about the residents in that community and the residents don't have the power to control their political leaders, let alone criminals. Continuing along this line of reasoning, how much personal guilt do some residents accept about their neighborhood and would they see themselves as rundown and "empty?" Thus, crime is pervasive and an intricate part of the culture, and therefore, social order existed less often than social disorder.

Keep in mind, too, that community centered programs (as opposed to a philosophy) are administratively tugged neatly into incident-driven enforcement units. Administratively it makes sense that personnel need to be deployed through a systematic method of command and that command must have access to personnel to make decisions about deployment especially as events change daily within a neighborhood. Yet, officers who perform community tasks on a hit and miss basis might view the assignment differently as might community members who realize community officers are merely "slumming" in those assignments. "It isn't really police work," wrote a community resident who was also a Sacramento police officer.

Using the SPD's strategic goals as part of the above rationale, for example: the SPD developed a plan, they carried out, and they conducted the training, the education, coordination, and evaluation. In what way were community members involved other than to accept the dictates of the SPD?

Also, the SPD has moved in a direction of empowered partnerships, but those partnerships seem to be among other justice agencies. Those partnerships may not be as welcomed by the community as the SPD leads us to believe. For instance, the survey revealed the residents do not feel safe in their own community or their homes and that there has been little change in how they feel about safety as compared to the proceeding year. Safety issues to homeowners, among other issues, seem to relate to confidence levels of the police. And although they reported that SPD performance is professional, the highest percent (82%) of the sample (even when compared to the other eight jurisdictions) revealed they wanted control over police (not city) oversight committees as an answer to crime control in Sacramento. An appropriate question might be: How trustworthy are the police? Granted, it may be only this sample's perspective, but what do those individuals think who didn't take the survey? What about those who might not want to attend community meetings for whatever reason? Have they given up on the cops? Yet, it must be pointed out that the SPD is operating with fewer police officers per one thousand of the population than 5 and even 10 years ago.

The SPD's Website reports that SPD delivers quality police service. And, there's evidence that their rank and file are hard working officers who posses integrity and honor. But policy seems to be another matter. Missing from many of their equations are the decisions developed by community members.

ENDNOTES

1. See Sacramento's Website at http://www. sacpd.org

2. Demographically, as of December 1999, the SPD employs 71% white officers, 7% African American officers, 12% Hispanic offices, 2% Filipino officers, and 8% Asian officers (source: SPD's Website).

3. Source: SPD's Website.

4. Source: SPD's Website.

5. All of Sacramento's neighborhood associations are viewable on-line at http://www. sacto.org/ns/na/nad2.htm; it should be mentioned that some of these associations aided in distributing, collecting, and returning the survey for this investigation. As a matter of confidentiality, of course, those association names are withheld at their request.

6. Available at http://www.sacto.org/ns/na/ mansion.htm.

7. Captain Steve Segura and Nancy Boemer-Otis of the SPD supplied much of the data and narrative for this section of the chapter.

8. The complete report is available at http:// www.sacto.org/cityman/OPA2000.pdf.

9.

City	Population	Sworn Officers
Sacramento	405,963	650
Oakland	402,104	701
Long Beach	457,608	860
Fresno	420,594	701

(*Source:* Office of Police Accountability, Sacramento Police Department, p. 39. On-line http:// www.sacto.org/cityman/OPA2000.pdf.)

10. The CSUP employs 15 full-time sworn officers.

11. Some of the surveys were distributed by university students at community meetings in the East Sacramento area, and some university students distributed surveys in other parts of the city. To insure confidentiality, the names of the students and the community meeting where the surveys were distributed were known only by the university instructors who aided the principal researcher.

12. See Bureau of Justice Statistics (1997). And it is suggested that you use caution in that Total Crime Index rates are not necessarily reliable methods when comparing various cities due to a large number of variables that impact crime.

CHAPTER 11

CONCLUSION
AND RECOMMENDATIONS

REVIEW

The ideas investigated asked the question of 2,010 survey takers and 76 interviewees: does police practice enhance neighborhood safety issues and provide social order or stability? It was believed that community police strategies give rise to crime control, reductions in the fear of crime, and enhancements in resident quality of life experiences. There were certain assumptions held by the principal investigator which were that if community members, especially culturally diverse members, influenced the decisions of the police, the greater the likelihood that public safety and lifestyle experiences would be enhanced. It was believed that in effect, the community, especially culturally diverse communities, should be active in policing themselves and accept more responsibility for crime and their own quality of life issues because the police can not control crime, reduce the fear of crime, and enhance lifestyle experiences themselves, nor should they.

Although specific findings were revealed in previous chapters, one conclusion an observer might reach now after reviewing the evidence is that:

Although residents attended meetings, there is little evidence that they influenced police decision-making processes at any level.

Furthermore:

There was little support that community members regardless of their cultural diversity influenced police practice. Therefore, social order was not necessarily enhanced through community police efforts in any of the jurisdictions tested.

Yet, it should be clear that levels of social order in the 21st century are impacted by the police, but many societal attributes affect social order, too. For example, individual and collective historical and current events, economic and health experiences, and cultural and religious beliefs can change an entire nation's way of life almost overnight. Technology, politics, and the weather—including the fullness of the moon—can alter social order levels, too. Lest we forget, sporting events and municipal and state services of all variations from water, to zoning and licensing, to health care play major roles in public order.

The evidence offered through police records celebrating enforcement and embracing the use of force allegedly toward social order and the information offered in this investigation imply a compelling argument that the police largely maintain the interests of the dominant class. American police service is centered in obsolete methods of social control linked to western European ideals of maintaining class interests. Of course, the rationale is that social control provides social order. But all through the history of policing, the contradiction of control and order has depended on who's defining what. In this case, the evidence suggests Eurocentric perspectives define the standards of social order in the United States. But many Americans find that perspective inappropriate and un-American, and now they are joined by many other individuals, many from other countries, who want to succeed in America. Rather than finding the police as providers of safety and leaders of democracy, they see something else. They find isolation, discrimination, and fear of the police to be more commonplace than expected. It is odd that even in the jurisdictions investigated in which a person of color was the top police executive in that police agency (i.e., Columbia, Columbus, Miami-Dade County, Sacramento), participants seem to say that they were neglected and discriminated against by both police services and municipal services. The function of policing must be a means to justice and to the sanctity of individual liberty. American police have done a fine job all things considered, but the challenge changes on a daily basis. A thumbnail view of the findings will help formulate your conclusions about law and order.

HIGHLIGHTING FINDINGS

Alexandria

1. Police and municipal agencies provided lip-service as opposed to quality services.
2. Community sees police and municipal lip-service as intentional.
3. Community demands reliable and full information.
4. Gangs and juveniles and fear or lack of trust of the police were two serious community problem issues.
5. Remedies were quality policing and municipal services.
6. Participants felt they were entitled to more city services than other residents.
7. Businesses should reflect morality and values of constituents and those that don't should be closed.

Boston

1. The most serious community problems were street drug activity and home invasion/carjacking.
2. Fear or lack of trust of police was one leading problem among residents in some Boston communities and all participants interviewed.
3. Remedies of most serious community problems related to quality city services first and police services, including strict enforcement and arrest, second.
4. Participants perceived obligation of police to solve neighborhood issues including marginal businesses, abandoned and dangerous buildings, opportunities to find suitable living accommodations and opportunities to purchase homes, and crime issues, especially that of controlling youth.
5. Participants perceived criminals as those with "criminal intent" to harm others and placed slum and business owners into a "criminal" classification.
6. Municipal agencies and Boston government had their own vested interests and those interests were not grounded in the community.
7. The participants trusted police more than politicians.
8. Because police policy changed often (due to the politicians), some didn't have confidence in police practice.
9. They wanted police to take control of city services.
10. Optimally, they would provide input about neighborhood requirements to the police and the police would provide all of the services of the city.
11. They wanted less responsibility for enhancing their communities.
12. Newcomers felt disenfranchised with municipal and police services.
13. Newcomers felt discriminated against in housing, jobs, and schools (children, too).

Columbia

1. There was more disorder than order because of lack of information and knowledge about how public agencies work (i.e., police, health care, and public transportation).
2. Community members were subject to justice sanctions more often.
3. Participants were suspicious of police supervision over their children.
4. Involvement of church and police opened doors of concern (but it seems to work in Columbia, at least from the perspective of the CPD).
5. A good relationship existed between individual officers and community members.
6. Gangs and juveniles issues and street drug activity were seen as the two most serious community problems.
7. Quality policing and municipal services were seen as the best remedies.
8. A luck of understanding about how the justice system and city government worked was observed.

Columbus

1. Inconsistent policing and municipal services were perceived.
2. Information was thought to be manipulated by police agency.
3. There was a consensus that participants should receive most of the municipal services (instead of others).
   a. they felt entitled
   b. "fairness" and equality were two different concepts
4. There was a sense of uncertainty in responses.
   a. resentment and perhaps alienation were felt
5. Home invasion and street drug activity were seen as the most serious community problems.
6. Quality city services were seen as the answer to community problems.
7. Participants felt entitled to more municipal services than other residents.

Miami-Dade

1. The community had few problems with police as an institution.
2. The community rejected individual officers who rejected diversity of community.
3. Municipal services were major issues.
4. Residents were not interested in assimilating into American culture (proud of their own).
   a. they were not anti-American
   b. mainstream America seen as an irresponsible drug culture lacking moral stability and protected by the police
5. School curriculum should foster community cultural perspectives.
6. Home invasions and streets, lights, empty buildings, and graffiti issues were primary community problems.
7. Remedies included quality policing and municipal services and home ownership and business investment issues.
8. Police investigators lacked cultural experience of community and often made wrongful arrests of citizens. As a result, crime was reported less often.

Midland

1. Issues centered around a mistrust of municipal and police policy.
2. Participants felt they received lip-service on municipal and police matters.
3. They took pride in neighborhoods and homes.
4. They experienced feelings of isolation.
5. They felt deprived of services delivered throughout the city.

6. They sought police guidance of their youth in understanding the law in a safe environment.
7. They rejected police enforcement of their children.
8. Their properties were in need of repair, and they were denied a home equity loan to aid them in that repair because their property was in need of repair.
9. Fear or lack of trust of police and home invasion were seen as the most serious community problems.
10. Home ownership issues and business investment were seen as remedies.
11. There was a lack of understanding of justice community and municipal services.

Palm Beach County

1. Police agency lacked a uniform philosophy.
2. There were inconsistent problem-solving strategies.
3. Programs and problem-solving were under police command.
4. Specific communities were targeted for community policing initiatives.
5. Programs were centered in police issues as opposed to neighborhood issues.
6. Information was not shared, knowledge of system was not articulated.
7. Community problems were seen as streets, lights, empty buildings, and graffiti issues, and street drug activity.
8. Remedies for community problems included quality policing and municipal services, and youth supervision and enforced curfews.
9. There was a high resident turnover.

Sacramento

1. The police advanced their police organization in several ways.
   a. they formed partnerships with other justice agencies
   b. they developed strategic goals
   c. they created police programs as opposed to community programs
2. There was an exceptional willingness of the community to contribute to police decision-making processes.
3. People who declared another homeland than the USA felt neglected by municipal and police service.
4. Police operated with fewer officers than in previous years.
5. Streets, lights, empty buildings, and graffiti issues and fear or lack of trust of police were two of the most serious community problems.
6. Home ownership and business investment were remedies for community problems.
7. Residents blamed themselves for their lifestyle conditions.
8. They felt that if they were heard, leaders would "do the right thing."

WHEN THINKING ABOUT POLICE
PRACTICE BASED ON THE EVIDENCE

With all of these thoughts in mind and the compelling evidence offered among the preceding chapters and the information in *Applied Community Policing in the 21st Century,* the following items should come to mind when thinking about police efforts to control crime, reduce the fear of crime, and enhance constituent lifestyles.[1]

- Social order or stability is the primary goal of American society
- The primary function of American police is to defend constitutional guarantees to enhance social order
- The best method to reach this function is through community police strategies
- Community police concepts exist in different forms
- Eurocentric values and goals influence police practice
- Dominant class interests are protected through Eurocentric practices
- Police should be facilitative leaders in their jurisdictions
- Municipal services should come under the authority of the police
- Problem-solving strategies should be emphasized in all jurisdictional services
- Community and officers must be provided information about jurisdictional services
- Community and officers must be trained to identify and resolve community concerns
- Community members and community officers must be empowered to resolve issues leading to crime, reducing fear and enhancing lifestyles
- Groups that do not or can not participate in community meetings must be heard
- Community officers do not have to be sworn officers

It comes down the idea, and granted it is a difficult idea to consider, that enforcement of the law is not the most important influence impacting social order. Enforcement is important and necessary, and should it be ignored crime would increase in both frequency and intensity. However, selective enforcement might be one avenue that makes sense; that is, sworn officers should only be involved with crimes of violence, and other nonenforcement or personnel accidents handled by others.

Additionally, the general lack of knowledge was apparent in a high percent of the responses, suggesting that police agencies have a bigger challenge than they expected. Due to this lack of knowledge about local events and police and jurisdictional services, most constituents felt alienated or uncertain about police intentions. Then, too, realizing that many community members blamed themselves for their condition was unexpected. As a result, accepting the label of "loser" might have a lot to do with some of their lifestyle decisions.

On the other hand, some community members thought they were far better than most residents and should receive the lion's share of city resources. In a final analysis, one realization is that whatever direction is pursued by local government or their agencies, such as the police department, residents will be less likely to be satisfied unless they accept the responsibility of managing their communities through problem-solving strategies in collaboration with the local services including the police. The task is to move crime control, reduction of fear, and enhancement of lifestyles into the hands of those who will benefit the most: the community members themselves. In part, police leadership can lighten their load once they provide the leadership for services that impact social order—jurisdictional amenities such as health clinics, transportation, street repair, and so on.

It is also clear that through the eyes of the American public police as a whole are not regarded as highly as their responsibilities. The American public wants change, yet there is disagreement about what change might be required. That might be due, in part, to a lack of knowledge about police work since often the media tends to offer the media's version of it, which can amount to good entertainment.[2] When police practice meets community standards judiciously, the community is generally satisfied and most community members attempt to comply with standards and the directives of the police through police personnel. Therefore, the community will support the police when the community feels police power mirrors their own ideals. As a result, law and order are upheld without the use of force and the police will no longer be viewed "as the most visible symbol of the most negative elements of government."

In other words, the police must become part of the democratic process and assume more responsibility for their jobs. Since the primary function of the American police is to safeguard the Constitution of the United States and to exercise due process guarantees to all the individuals whom they serve, their values and delivery system must change, too. For instance, some of those changes include the elimination of the "criminalization of poverty" notions which justify the targeting of challenged neighborhoods by enforcement agencies. They need to reshape the values of police culture that takes its cue from Eurocentric (Western European) perspectives to a more modern perspective in keeping with the populations they serve.[3]

Frankly, in the 21st century, the function of the police must change or it will doom itself to primary deployment of an inner-city enforcement unit of radicals who oppose the status quo since American policing tends to defend the dominant class more often than others. One way of preventing police extinction in a democratic society is to bring certainty to its constituents and respect to its contributions by aiding constituents through facilitative leadership that will educate community members and municipal personnel to make the right choices. Yet, make no mistake, the community must become accountable and responsible for appropriate community advancement, too.

Finally, although this work's sister book *Applied Community Policing in the 21st Century* discusses the events of September 11th in some depth, it bears brief mention here. Those events have left us with feelings of uncertainty, anger, and, for some of us, sorrow—and rightfully so. Another response is from some law enforcement experts who have suggested that the Airline Pilots Union is the model for self-defense against terrorists—guns in the cockpit.[4] Furthermore, further attacks at a sporting event, for instance, should be met with police firepower. That is, "Let us pray that if this happens we [police] will be there to stop it before the body count gets too high. The terrorists will probably wear body armor, so think about headshots. And they will probably have accomplices, so don't let your guard down after you shoot the first one" (Grossman, 2001, page 117). Draw your own implications of this statement and while you're doing it think about others who used a similar perspective such as Idi Amin, Pol Pot, and—if those names don't ring any bells—try Adolph Hitler or Stalin or Birmingham, Watts, and Kent State. Consider that one of the greatest fortifications police agencies and communities can build to defend America is problem solving partnerships. There are a number of ways that a community partnerships can help, for example, mutually deciding on potential targets in the community and "legal" methods of protecting those targets, Protecting America also means protecting the law—it is denial of due process and our freedom that our enemies want to destroy more than any other American possesion. The best way to practice freedom is through empowered community partnerships.

ENDNOTES

1. All conclusions and representations in this work as well as in *Applied Community Policing in the 21st Century* are the final analyses and interpretations made by the principal investigator.

2. See *Applied Community Policing in the 21st Century*, Chapter 2 for more details about this idea.

3. Ibid.

4. See Grossman, D. (2001, December). Terrrorism and local police, *Law and Order, 49(12)*, 117.

BIBLIOGRAPHY

Berger, P. L. (1963). *Invitation to sociology: A humanistic perspective.* Garden City, NJ: Anchor Books.

Brodeur, J. P. (1998). *How to recognize good policing: Problems and issues.* Thousand Oaks, CA: Sage Publications.

Bureau of Justice Statistics. (2001). *Sourcebook of Criminal Statistics 2000.* [Online]. Available: http://www.ojp.usdoj.gov/bjs/

Cardarelli, A. P., McDevitt, J., & Baum, K. (1998). The rhetoric and reality of community policing in small and medium sized cities and towns. *Policing: An International Journal of Police Strategies & Management, 21(3),* 397–415.

Carter, D. L., & Radelet, L. A. (1999). *The police and the community, 6th edition.* Upper Saddle River, NJ: Prentice Hall.

Citta, J. (1996). Police department surveys to help police officers grow. [On-line]. Available: www.communitypolicing.org

DuBois, J., & Hartnett, S. M. (2002). Making the community side of community policing work: What needs to be done. In Dennis J. Stevens (Ed.), *Policing and community policing.* Upper Saddle River, NJ: Prentice Hall.

Dutton, D. (1998, May). Don't forget to ask your customers what's most important to them. [On-line]. Available: www.communitypolicing.com

Eck, J. E., & LaVigne, N. G. (1994). *Using research: A primer for law enforcement managers.* Washington, DC: Police Executive Research Forum.

Ericson, R. V., & Haggerty, K. D. (1997). *Policing the risk society.* Toronto: University of Toronto Press.

Ferguson, C. U. (2002) Creative community policing initiatives in Columbia, South Carolina. In Dennis J. Stevens (Ed.), *Communities and policing* (pp. 45–76). Upper Saddle River, NJ: Prentice Hall.

Goldstein, H. (1977). *Policing a free society.* Cambridge, MA: Ballinger.

Goldstein, H. (1990). *Problem-oriented policing.* New York: McGraw-Hill.

Kelling, G. (1998). Columbia's comprehensive communities program: A case study. Provided by the Columbia South Carolina Police Department from their archives.

Kelling, G. L., & Moore, M. H. (1999). The evolving strategy of policing. In Victor E. Kappeler (Ed.), *The police and society* (pp. 2–26). Prospect Heights, IL: Waveland Press.

Kirkland, R., & Glensor, R. (1992). Community oriented policing and problem solving department report. Reno, NV: Reno Police Department.

Masterson, M., & Stevens, D. J. (2002). The value of measuring community policing performance in Madison, Wisconsin. In Dennis J. Stevens (Ed.), *Policing and community partnerships* (pp. 77–92). Upper Saddle River, NJ: Prentice Hall.

Masterson, M., & Stevens, D. J. (2001, December). Madison speaks up: Measuring community policing performance. *Law and Order, 49(10),* 98–100.

Nowicki, D. E. (1998). Mixed messages. In Geoffrey Alpert and Alex Piquero (Eds.), *Community policing* (pp. 265–274). Prospect Heights, IL: Waveland Press.

Oettmeier, T. N., & Wycoff, M. A. (1997). Personnel performance evaluations in the community policing context. In Geoffrey Alpert and Alex Piquero

(Eds.), *Community policing* (pp. 275–306). Prospect Heights, IL: Waveland Press.

Peel Regional Police Survey of Attitudes and Opinions. (1994, March). Brampton, Ontario: Benchmark Study.

Skogan, W. G. (1990). *Disorder and decline: Crime and the spiral of decay in American neighborhoods*. New York: The Free Press.

Skogan, W. G. (1998). Community participation and community policing. In Jean-Paul Brodeur (Ed.), *How to recognize good policing: Problems and issues* (pp. 88–106). Thousand Oaks, CA: Sage Publications.

Skogan, W. G., & Hartnett, S. M. (1997). *Community policing: Chicago style*. New York: Oxford University Press.

Stephens, D. W. (1996). *Community problem oriented policing: Measuring impact, quantifying quality in policing*. Washington, DC: Police Executive Research Forum.

Stevens, D. J. (1998a). What do law enforcement officers think about their work? *The Law Enforcement Journal, 5*(1), 60–62.

———. (1998b). Urban communities and homicide: Why American blacks resort to murder. *Police and Society, 8,* 253–267.

———. (1998c). Incarcerated women, crime, and drug addiction. *The Criminologist, 22*(1), 3–14.

———. (1999a). Do college educated officers provide quality police service? *Law and Order,* December, *47*(12), 37–41.

———. (1999b). Corruption among narcotic officers: A study of innocence and integrity. *Journal of Police and Criminal Psychology,* Fall, *14*(2), 1–11.

———. (1999c). American police resolutions. *Police Journal, LXXII*(2): 140–150.

———. (1999d, March). Police tactical units and community response. *Law and Order, 47*(3), 48–52.

———. (1999e). Interviews with women convicted of murder: Battered women syndrome revisited. *International Review of Victimology, 6*(2).

———. (2000, October). Improving community policing: Using managerial style and total quality management. *Law and Order,* 197–204.

———. (2001a). *Case studies in community policing.* Upper Saddle River, NJ: Prentice Hall.

———. (2001b, May). Civil liabilities and selective enforcement. *Law and Order, 49*(5), 105–109.

———. (2001c). Community policing and managerial techniques: Total quality management techniques. *The Police Journal, 74*(1), 26–41.

———. (2001d). *Measuring performance: An easy guide to master the skills of a researcher.* NY: Authors Choice.

———. (Ed.). (2002a). *Policing and community partnerships.* Upper Saddle River, NJ: Prentice Hall.

———. (2002b). Civil liabilities and arrest decisions. In Jeffery T. Walker (Ed.), *Policing and the law.* (pp. 53–70), Upper Saddle River, NJ: Prentice Hall.

———. (2002c). *Inside the mind of sexual offenders: Predatory rapists, pedophiles, and criminal profiles.* New York: Authors Choice Press.

———. (2003). *Applied community policing in the 21st century.* Boston, MA: Allyn & Bacon.

Stevens, D. J., & Ward, C. (1997). College education and recidivism: Educating criminals is meritorious. *Journal of Correctional Education, 48*(3), 106–111.

Stevens, P., & Yach, D. M. (1996). *Community policing in action: A practitioner's guide.* Kenwyn: Juta.

Stewart-Brown, R., & Rosario, M. (2001, November/December). Mind your own business is bad advice. *Community Policing Exchange, VII*(33), 1, 8.

Surveys of citizen attitudes. (1995). Telemasp Bulletin. Huntsville, Texas: Texas Law Enforcement Management and

Administrative Problem, Bill Blackwood Enforcement Management Institute of Texas.

Thurman, Q., & McGarrell, E. F. (1995, June). Findings of the 1994 Spokane Police Department Citizen Survey: Final report, Washington State Institute for Community Oriented Policing, Spokane, Washington.

Trojanowicz, R. C. (1982). *An evaluation of the neighborhood foot patrol program in Flint, Michigan.* East Lansing: Department of Criminal Justice, Michigan State University.

Trojanowicz, R. C., & Carter, D. L. (1988). *The philosophy and role of community policing.* East Lansing: National Neighborhood Foot Patrol Center, Michigan State University.

Trojanowicz, R. C., & Dixon, S. L. (1974). *Criminal justice and the community.* Englewood Cliffs, NJ: Prentice Hall.

Thurman, Q., & McGarrell, E. F. (1995, June). Findings of the 1994 Spokane Police Department Citizen Survey: Final report, Washington State Institute for Community Oriented Policing, Spokane, Washington.

US Census, 2000. [On-line]. Available: http://www.census.gov

Wilson, J. Q., & Kelling, G. L. (2000). Broken windows: The police and neighborhood safety. In Willard M. Oliver (Ed.), *Community policing: Classical readings* (pp. 1–15). Upper Saddle River, NJ: Prentice Hall.